D1602141

THE THERAPIST'S NOTEBOOK on POSITIVE PSYCHOLOGY

THE THERAPIST'S NOTEBOOK on POSITIVE PSYCHOLOGY

Activities, Exercises, and Handouts

BILL O'HANLON
BOB BERTOLINO

Routledge
Taylor & Francis Group
New York London

Routledge
Taylor & Francis Group
711 Third Avenue
New York, NY 10017

Routledge
Taylor & Francis Group
27 Church Road
Hove, East Sussex BN3 2FA

© 2012 by Taylor and Francis Group, LLC
Routledge is an imprint of Taylor & Francis Group, an Informa business

Printed in the United States of America on acid-free paper

International Standard Book Number: 978-0-415-88750-2 (Paperback)

For permission to photocopy or use material electronically from this work, please access www.copyright.com (http://www.copyright.com/) contact the Copyright Clearance Center, Inc. (CCC), 222 Rosewood Drive, Danvers, MA 01923, 978-750-8400. CCC is a not-for-profit organizatic that provides licenses and registration for a variety of users. For organizations that have been granted a photocopy license by the CCC, a separat system of payment has been arranged.

Trademark Notice: Product or corporate names may be trademarks or registered trademarks, and are used only for identification and explanatic without intent to infringe.

Library of Congress Cataloging-in-Publication Data

O'Hanlon, William Hudson.
  The therapist's notebook on positive psychology : activities, exercises, and handouts / Bill O'Hanlon & Bob Bertolino.
    p. cm.
  Includes bibliographical references and index.
  ISBN 978-0-415-88750-2 (pbk. : alk. paper)
  1. Positive psychology. 2. Psychotherapy. I. Bertolino, Bob, 1965- II. Title.

BF204.6.O43 2011
150.19'88--dc22   2011001065

Visit the Taylor & Francis Web site at
http://www.taylorandfrancis.com

and the Routledge Web site at
http://www.routledgementalhealth.com

To Helen and Rudy, who have contributed to my positive psychology. And to Glenn and Beth Hendrickson, who have shown me kindness, trust, and acceptance.

Bill O'Hanlon

To Misha, Morgan, and Claire. The world is wonderful with you.

Bob Bertolino

Contents

Acknowledgments

Thanks to Bob Bertolino for initiating this project and bringing his usual attention to detail and amazing work ethic to it.

Bill O'Hanlon

Thank you to my colleagues and students at Maryville University and to the staff and clients of Youth In Need, Inc., who inspire me every day. To Bill O'Hanlon, thank you for years of friendship, support, and for your unwavering passion to change things that need changing.

Bob Bertolino

From both of us: Thank you to all the researchers in positive psychology, behavioral economics, and other fields who provided the raw material from which to work. And a very special thank you to George Zimmar, Marta Moldvai, and the entire Routledge family for embracing this book and for our ongoing collaborative partnership.

Introduction

In 1991, Jerry and Monique Sternin, experienced anti-poverty workers, were hired by the charitable organization Save the Children to create a large-scale effective program to reduce child malnutrition in Vietnam. More than 65% of Vietnamese children were malnourished at the time. The couple was given an essentially impossible task. They had a small budget as Save the Children was starving financially. Many other relief agencies had tried previously to accomplish this monumental task, and while they sometimes got short-term results, the rate for child malnutrition had remained stubbornly high.

Out of desperation, the Sternins decided to try a new approach. Working with four poor rural communities and 2,000 children under the age of three, the Sternins invited the community to identify poor families who had managed to avoid malnutrition despite all odds, facing the same challenges and obstacles as their neighbors and without access to any special resources. These families were what they called the "positive deviants." They were "positive" because they were doing things that worked, and "deviants" because they engaged in behaviors that most others did not (Pascale, Sternin, & Sternin, 2010).

The Sternins and the community, after observation and discussion, together discovered that caregivers in the Positive Deviant families collected tiny shrimps and crabs from paddy fields, and added those, along with sweet potato greens, to their children's meals. These foods were accessible to everyone, but most community members believed they were inappropriate for young children. The Positive Deviant families were also feeding their children small meals three to four times a day, rather than bigger meals twice a day, which was customary in that part of the world.

After this discovery, the remainder of the community changed its behavior to match that of the Positive Deviants, resulting in a rapid decrease in malnutrition in the four villages. Once word of the success of this effort spread, many other villages sent representatives to learn the approach, resulting in a significant decrease in child malnutrition rates that lasted over time in Vietnam. Within two years, malnutrition rates had dropped between 65 and 85% in every village the Sternins had visited.

We tell you this story to introduce you to a different way of thinking and approaching issues in psychotherapy. Psychotherapy has traditionally had a bias toward the problematic and pathological. In part, this is understandable. People come to us (or are referred) because they have problems. So the focus is on what is wrong. Part of this more negative bias comes from Freud and the early theories of psychology and psychotherapy. Freud wrote that the best one could expect in this life is "ordinary misery," and he considered the quest for more positive states of mind such as happiness or joy to be infantile wishes that could never be fulfilled.

Psychology also had a bias for studying negative states and conditions in human life. In their survey, psychologists/researchers David Myers and Ed Diener (1995) found that psychological publications and studies dealing with negative states outnumbered those examining positive states by a ratio of 17 to 1. Mihaly Csikszentmihalyi and Martin Seligman, former president of the American Psychological Association, echoed the need for research on positive states and well-being:

> What we have learned over 50 years is that the disease model does not move us closer to the prevention of these serious problems. Indeed the major strides in prevention have largely come from a perspective focused on systematically building competency, not correcting weakness. Prevention researchers have discovered that there are human strengths that act as buffers

against mental illness: courage, future-mindedness, optimism, interpersonal skill, faith, work ethic, hope, honesty, perseverance, the capacity for flow and insight, to name several. Much of the task of prevention in this new century will be to create a science of human strength whose mission will be to understand and learn how to foster these virtues in young people. Working exclusively on personal weakness and on the damaged brains, however, has rendered science poorly equipped to do effective prevention. We need now to call for massive research on human strength and virtue. We need to ask practitioners to recognize that much of the best work they already do in the consulting room is to amplify strengths rather than repair the weaknesses of their clients. (Seligman & Csikszentmihalyi, 2000, pp. 6–7)

In the early 1980s, Bill O'Hanlon, influenced by the work of psychiatrist Milton Erickson, created an approach to psychotherapy called Solution-Oriented Therapy. He presented a paper on that subject in 1986 at an Erickson Foundation conference (O'Hanlon, 1988). This new approach asserted that helping people discover their strengths, competencies, and indigenous solutions might be a more effective and more rapid approach to change (O'Hanlon & Weiner-Davis, 1989, 2003). Because people already had solutions and strengths but were not applying them, no new skills needed to be taught or mastered. No outside values were imposed. Instead of giving people outside knowledge from an expert, they could change using evoked abilities and resources from within them and their social environments. Soon after, Steve de Shazer and Insoo Kim Berg created their "solution-focused brief therapy" approach, which has since spread far and wide (Berg, 1991; Berg & Miller, 1992; De Shazer, 1985, 1988, 1991). Several other approaches emerged that were nonpathologically based and worked to evoke resources rather than focus on problems and pathology, notably Michael White and David Epston's Narrative Therapy (Epston, 1989; Epston & White, 1992; White, 1989; White & Epston, 1990) and Harry Goolishian and Harlene Anderson's Collaborative Language Systems approach (Anderson & Goolishian, 1988, 1992).

As the field of psychotherapy shifted to focus on strengths, a similar effort was underway in psychology research. Researchers Martin Seligman (1991, 2002), Chris Peterson, (2006), Mihaly Csikszentmihalyi (1990, 1996), Barbara Fredrickson (2009), Sonja Lyubomirsky (2008), Ed Diener (Diener & Biswas-Diener, 2008), and others began to connect and set an agenda to correct the overbalanced research into negative states and qualities and to encourage the study of positive emotions and what works in human life. This field of study came to be known as Positive Psychology.

The story we heard was that Martin Seligman was cranky with his daughter one day and she said to him, "Daddy, do you remember when I turned four and had to give up my blankey that I'd been carrying all my life?" "Yes," he answered. "Well, that was really hard to do, Daddy. If I can give up my blankey, you can give up being cranky." Sufficiently chastised and being a research psychologist, he searched the databases for research on how to become happier and more good-natured, and was made even more cranky when he could find very little of that kind of research. He became a man with a mission then and brought together various researchers, ran for president of the American Psychological Association, and helped divert grant and research money into this newly named and consolidated area of Positive Psychology.

Seligman and Csikszentmihalyi (2000, p. 5) have described Positive Psychology as concerned with documenting "what kinds of families result in children who flourish, what work settings support the greatest satisfaction among workers, what policies result in the strongest civic engagement, and how people's lives can be most worth living." Proponents posit that the study of the aforementioned areas would lead to improved understanding of individual, family, and community well-being and form the scientific basis for interventions to build thriving in those aspects of life. More recently, Seligman (2009) has described Positive Psychology as concerning itself with four primary areas:

1. Positive emotion and well-being
2. Meaning and purpose

3. Positive relationships
4. Positive accomplishments

It is important to note that Positive Psychology is not intended to replace traditional psychology. Instead, it is focused on building factors such as resilience, coping skills, protective factors, and strengths so that people may not just face and manage the problems of life but flourish in their everyday existence. To build capacity, Positive Psychology emphasizes the following areas:

- Positive attitudes and emotions
- Life satisfaction
- Loving and pleasant friendships and love relationships
- Engaging and meaningful activities and work
- Spirituality and meaning in life
- The importance of values and life goals that might help achieve or optimize them
- Kindness and compassion
- Hope
- Optimism
- Forgiveness
- Gratitude
- Contentment

To get you into the spirit of the book, we would like you to take a moment, stop reading, and do an inner activity.

Think of the awe-inspired and happiest moments of your life: when you saw an amazing sunset or got to the top of a mountain or fell in love or met your newborn for the first time. When you read a book or heard some music that moved you deeply. When you experienced a profound spiritual connection or moment. When you got some unexpectedly good news.

Use these moments to investigate how happiness happens for you, both the circumstances and your experience. Happiness is a subjective sense and we want you to at least have a grounding in your experience of it before you read on.

More and more compelling research continues to be done into the healthy and pleasant sides of human life. But this is only research, and many of you who are reading this book are primarily psychotherapists. Most of these researchers are, by their own admission, not therapists. So, the question is: How can we apply this recent research in Positive Psychology to clinical work to help people change in positive directions?

And that is the focus of this book. We have summarized and distilled the best of the field of Positive Psychology and allied research areas and translated those research findings into possible interventions that psychotherapists could use to help clients and patients. We have also highlighted several specific, robust findings from the psychotherapy literature that underscore the importance of focusing on strengths, meaning and purpose, connection, and well-being. In essence, this book delves into the emerging field of *Positive Psychotherapy*—representing a bridge between Positive Psychology and Psychotherapy, which have existed historically as two distinct and separate fields of study (Seligman, Rashid, & Parks, 2006). This book represents a new beginning for therapists, who after years of being known as "mental health professionals" but really focusing on mental illness and problems, can finally fulfill this label and focus on mental, behavioral, emotional, cognitive, and spiritual health.

The exercises in this book follow a standard format so they will be easy to use and implement. First, we name the exercise and provide an overview of it. Then we give some suggestions for when and how you might use the exercise, followed by the exercise itself. Occasionally, we add some sections that don't strictly fall into the exercise format and, for those, we will use separate sections sprinkled throughout the text.

It is important to keep several things in mind when using the exercises in this book. First, many of these research findings are preliminary and unreplicated. Some of them are correlational and not experimentally based and should be taken with a grain of salt. Next, with few exceptions, most of the exercises that have been studied scientifically through randomized clinical trials (RCTs) do not in and of themselves increase levels of happiness beyond a period of about one month. Said differently, the exercises such as the ones in this book frequently lead to immediate spikes of happiness but more often than not these boosts are short-lived. This is at least in part due to people not continuing to do the exercises that contributed to the increases in happiness. In addition, a good number of the studies on Positive Psychotherapy exercises to date have been Internet-based. In other words, there has been little to no involvement of mental health professionals in these studies other than collecting and interpreting the results of the exercises.

To address the various shortcomings of the available research, we recommend the following four general guidelines for therapists using the exercises in this book:

1. *Focus on fundamental skills such as listening, attending, and eliciting client feedback and respond to that feedback immediately as a means of strengthening the therapeutic relationship.* Researchers have identified several aspects of the alliance (i.e., empathy, positive regard, congruence) that are known to contribute to better alliances (see Norcross, 2002).
2. *Collaborate with clients on determining which exercises provide the best fit.* Numerous studies in psychotherapy have demonstrated the client's rating of the therapeutic alliance (i.e., the combination of client-therapist bond, collaboration with the client on goals, and collaboration with the client on tasks to accomplish those goals) as a reliable and consistent predictor of eventual treatment outcome (Bachelor & Horvath, 1999; Baldwin, Wampold, & Imel, 2007; Horvath & Bedi, 2002; Martin, Garske, & Davis, 2000; Orlinsky, Grawe, & Parks, 1994, Orlinksy, Rønnestad, & Willutzki, 2004).
3. *Encourage clients to use agreed-upon exercises in a routine and ongoing manner, continue those exercises that have proven beneficial, and experiment with new ones as needed.* In studies, researchers have found that people with the highest levels of happiness are the ones who maintain adherence to the exercises they were asked to try (Seligman, Steen, Park, & Peterson, 2005).
4. *Package exercises to increase the likelihood of benefit to clients.* It may not be practical for clients to do several exercises in a given day; however, it is suggested that therapists encourage clients to try more than one exercise and to do so on multiple occasions over an agreed-upon time frame. In doing so, it may be helpful to work with clients on a combination of exercises that can both contribute to an immediate boost in happiness and those that can be incorporated into everyday routines and provide longer-term satisfaction (Seligman et al., 2005).

You will discover, for particular clients, which, if any, of these exercises are helpful to them. And even if they do not produce any permanent positive shifts in happiness levels, perhaps they will help that client get a little traction out of their particular problem and suffering.

And now, with the "nuts and bolts" outlined, we leave you with another story, this one not from the world of relief but closer to home.

In the 1930s, a young girl named Gillian in England was sent to a psychologist for evaluation because she was disruptive in class. She regularly fidgeted, got up from her desk, talked to other classmates, and didn't focus on her work.

Her mother brought her to the psychologist and he tested her, spoke to her and her mother, and then asked Gillian to wait in his waiting room while he spoke with her mother in private. The psychologist told Gillian they would be a few minutes and, to keep her company and to help his discussion with her mother be more private, he turned on the radio in the waiting room. When the psychologist and the mother arrived in the office, the psychologist ushered the mother over to the door and had them both poke through the curtains to watch Gillian.

She was up and moving to the music. The psychologist turned to the mother and said, "Gillian isn't sick. She's a dancer. Take her to a dance school." And her mother did. There, Gillian discovered others much like her; people who couldn't sit still and had to move to think. She thrived in dance.

Gillian is Gillian Lynne. She was, for many years, a soloist at England's Royal Ballet Company, went on to found her own dance company and then to become a well-known choreographer. She choreographed Andrew Lloyd-Weber's *Cats*, *Phantom of the Opera*, and many other productions. She became a multi-millionaire.

These days, a psychologist would probably give Gillian a diagnosis of ADHD and recommend putting Gillian on medications so she could fit in better at school. Now we are not saying that those approaches are wrong or evil, only that they have become the mainstay of interventions in psychotherapy, with few alternatives.

This book offers an alternative. A research-based alternative. If it helps even one of your clients have a better course of therapy *and* experience more happiness, meaning, connection, or accomplishment, we will have done our job.

Bill O'Hanlon and Bob Bertolino, 2010

We know that because this field is evolving daily, more research and possibilities for clinical applications will be coming along after we have gone to print, so we have created a website that we will update and also offer supplemental materials to the book. Please visit: www.therapistsnotebookonpositivepsychology.com

References

Anderson, H., & Goolishian, H. (1988). Human systems as linguistic systems: Evolving ideas about the implications for theory and practice. *Family Process, 27*(4), 371–393.

Anderson, H., & Goolishian, H. (1992). The client is the expert: A not knowing approach to therapy. In S. McNamee & K. J. Gergen (Eds.), *Therapy as social construction* (pp. 25–39). Newbury Park, CA: Sage.

Bachelor, A., & Horvath, A. (1999). The therapeutic relationship. In S. D. Miller (Ed.), *The heart and soul of change*: *What works in therapy* (pp. 133–178). Washington, DC: American Psychological Association.

Baldwin, S. A., Wampold, B. E., & Imel, Z. E. (2007). Untangling the alliance-outcome correlation: Exploring the relative importance of therapist and patient variability in the alliance. *Journal of Consulting and Clinical Psychology, 75*(6), 842–852.

Berg, I. K. (1991). *Family preservation: A brief therapy workbook*. London: BT Press.

Berg, I. K., & Miller, S. D. (1992). *Working with the problem drinker: A solution-focused approach*. New York: Norton.

Csikszentmihalyi, M. (1996). *Creativity: Flow and the psychology of discovery and invention*. New York: HarperCollins.

Csikszentmihalyi, M. (1990). *Flow: The psychology of optimal experience*. New York: Harper & Row.

De Shazer, S. (1991). *Putting difference to work*. New York: Norton.

De Shazer, S. (1988). *Clues: Investigating solutions in brief therapy*. New York: Norton.

De Shazer, S. (1985). *Keys to solution in brief therapy*. New York: Norton.

Diener, E., & Biswas-Diener, R. (2008). *Happiness: Unlocking the mysteries of psychological health*. New York: Wiley-Blackwell.

Epston, D. (1989). *Collected papers*. Adelaide, South Australia: Dulwich Centre Publications.

Epston, D., & White, M. (1992). *Experience, contradiction, narrative, and imagination: Selected papers of David Epston and Michael White 1989–1991*. Adelaide, South Australia: Dulwich Centre Publications.

Fredrickson, B. (2009). *Positivity: Top-notch research reveals the 3 to 1 ratio that will change your life*. New York: Three Rivers Press.

Horvath, A. O., & Bedi, R. P. (2002). The alliance. In J. C. Norcross (Ed.), *Psychotherapy relationships that work: Therapist contributions and responsiveness to patient needs* (pp. 37–69). New York: Oxford University Press.

Lyubomirsky, S. (2008). *The how of happiness: A scientific approach to getting the life you want*. New York: Penguin.

Martin, D. J., Garske, J. P., & Davis, M. K. (2000). Relationship of the therapeutic alliance with outcome and other variables: A meta-analytic review. *Journal of Consulting and Clinical Psychology, 68*(3), 438–450.

Myers, D., & Diener, E. (1995). Who is happy? *Psychological Science, 6,* 10–19.

Norcross, J. C. (2002). *Psychotherapy relationships that work: Therapist contributions and responsiveness to patients*. New York: Oxford.

O'Hanlon, B. (1988). Solution-oriented therapy: A megatrend in psychotherapy. In J. Zeig, and S. Lankton, (Eds.), *Developing Ericksonian psychotherapy*, New York: Brunner/Mazel.

O'Hanlon, B., & Weiner-Davis, M. (1989). *In search of solutions: A new direction in psychotherapy*. New York: Norton.

O'Hanlon, B., & Weiner-Davis, M. (2003). *In search of solutions: A new direction in psychotherapy*. New York: Norton. [Revised paperback edition]

Orlinsky, D. E., Grawe, K., & Parks, B. K. (1994). Process and outcome in psychotherapy—noch einmal. In A. E. Bergin & S. L. Garfield (Eds.), *Handbook of psychotherapy and behavior change* (4th ed.) (pp. 270–378). New York: Wiley.

Orlinsky, D. E., Rønnestad, M. H., & Willutzki, U. (2004). Fifty years of process-outcome research: Continuity and change. In M. J. Lambert (Ed.), *Bergin and Garfield's handbook of psychotherapy and behavior change* (5th ed.) (pp. 307–390). New York: Wiley.

Pascale, R., Sternin, J., & Sternin, M. (2010). *The power of positive deviance: How unlikely innovators solve the world's toughest problems*. Boston, MA: Harvard Business Press.

Peterson, C. (2006). *A primer in positive psychology*. New York: Oxford.

Seligman, M. E. P. (2009). Advances in positive psychology. *The Evolution of Psychotherapy Conference*. Anaheim, CA: Milton H. Erickson Foundation.

Seligman, M. E. P. (2002). *Authentic happiness: Using the new positive psychology to realize your potential for lasting fulfillment*. New York: Free Press.

Seligman, M. E. P. (1991). *Learned optimism: How to change your mind and your life*. New York: Knopf.

Seligman, M. E. P., & Csikszentmihalyi, M. (2000). Positive psychology: An introduction. *American Psychologist, 55*(1), 5–14.

Seligman, M. E. P., Rashid, T., & Parks, A. C. (2006). Positive psychotherapy. *American Psychologist, 61*(8), 774–788.

Seligman, M. E. P., Steen, T. A., Park, N., & Peterson, C. (2005). Positive psychology progress: Empirical validation of interventions. *American Psychologist, 60*(5), 410–421.

White, M. (1989). *Selected papers*. Adelaide, South Australia: Dulwich Centre Publications.

White, M., & Epston, D. (1990). *Narrative means to therapeutic ends*. New York: Norton.

THE P.O.S.I.T.I.V.E. FRAMEWORK
From Research to Practice

Happiness: What We Know So Far from the Research

We begin here by highlighting a few points that underscore the activities and exercises in Chapter 1:

Most of us are bad at predicting what will make us happy.

We tend to overestimate the positive impact of having more money, more material objects, and good things happening to us will increase our happiness. We tend to overestimate the negative impact of having bad things happen to us.

Most of us are pretty happy.

And we tend to have stable happiness levels through life (this is often called our happiness set point), although most of us get a little happier as life goes on (and there is often a slight dip in happiness levels at mid-life). There are some things that can increase or decrease our general happiness levels for short or prolonged periods. Stress, anxiety, and depression can bring down the levels of happiness. We discuss this research throughout this book while relating it to clinical work.

Subjective well-being is a little different from happiness. It involves:

Satisfaction with life conditions
Experience frequent positive emotions
Experience infrequent negative emotions (Diener, 1984)

A certain percentage of our happiness/subjective well-being (some estimate 40%) can be changed by things we do and shifts in attention and attitude. Jonathan Haidt (2006) provides a nice formula in his book, *The Happiness Hypothesis*: $H = S + C + V$, where H is your general happiness level, S is your happiness set point, C is your life conditions, and V is your voluntary activities. *This last is the territory we cover in this book—the things you and your clients can do to affect happiness levels and one's sense of well-being.*

And perhaps we should give you a definition of happiness before diving in. There are many, of course, and no correct definitive on which all can agree, but for clarity and simplicity, we quite like this one:

Pleasure/Positive Emotions + Engagement + Meaning = Happiness

But mostly, of course, aside from definitions and formulas, most of us know when we are happy or satisfied quite well without any help from the scientists or theorists.

In this chapter we introduce the overall framework that we will use to organize the disparate material from Positive Psychology and allied areas of research. We provide at least one activity or exercise to use based on the particular area of focus or research finding.

While there have been some articles and even a book or two on psychotherapy approaches that derive from the findings in Positive Psychology, these were for the most part either unsatisfying to us because they didn't provide much practical guidance or specifics, or they were written by theorists or researchers.

Our primary guideline for translating this research is practicality and a realistic understanding of clinical work. Also, we don't expect you, the reader, to use every one of these exercises or activities. The book is divided into "bite-sized" pieces, making it easy to dip into one or the other of them and try them at random. Of course, if you prefer, you could read them through or try them out more systematically, but this is not necessary to get the value out of this volume.

If you have a background in more traditional approaches, this new emphasis may take some time to incorporate or shift into. It may take even more time for it to feel natural. That's okay. Our goal is not to make whatever you are currently doing obsolete (or wrong), but rather to supplement and expand your repertoire and viewpoint.

Approach these activities and exercises with openness, and you should be fine. Now, on to the first chapter and exercises.

References

Diener, E. (1984). Subjective well-being. *Psychological Bulletin*, *95*, 542–575.
Haidt, J. (2006). *The happiness hypothesis*. New York: Basic.

Clean Your Well-Being with S.O.A.P.

Overview

There is a lot of material in this book. We don't want you to get overwhelmed. To start things out and keep them simple, we offer a brief overview of the four key areas that have been shown in Positive Psychology research to have a significant impact on people's sense of well-being and happiness. We have organized the book with the mnemonic P.O.S.I.T.I.V.E., but for now let's make things even more memorable with the shorter mnemonic S.O.A.P.

S.O.A.P. stands for

S. = Social connections, probably the most neglected in our busy and isolated modern lives; if you have a rich social life (not busy, necessarily, just rich) and positive social connections, you will likely be happier.

O. = Optimism; if you approach life and troubles with a more optimistic explanatory style and attitude, you are more likely to be happy. Luckily, this is learnable.

A. = Appreciation/gratitude; if you can wake up to the wonders of the world and the blessings you have, you will likely find yourself being more satisfied in your life.

P. = Purpose/meaning; if you have the sense that your life is about something more than satisfying your personal needs and wants and you feel it has a bigger meaning and purpose, again, you are more likely to be satisfied.

Suggestions for Use

This exercise is primarily for you the therapist, although you are welcome to invite your clients to do it as well. It is designed to "get you into" the field of Positive Psychology, and give you an overview of where we are going in this book and some of the key concepts and activities that can make a difference in your clients' lives that derive from that field.

Exercise

To complete this exercise, please complete the following steps.

1. In the space below, list your significant social connections. This includes:

Friends _____

Romantic relationships _____

Friendly co-workers _____

Pets _____

Family members _____

Neighbors _____

Groups in which you have good connections with one or more members:

    Church congregations _____

    Choirs/musical groups _____

    Book groups _____

    Sports teams _____

Military units _____

Work groups _____

Professional organizations _____

Live or web-based interest groups _____

Self-help/support groups _____

Your extended family _____

[Fill in any other groups in your life that haven't been covered in this list]

2. Now, next to each entity on the list in Step 1, make a note of how often you get together with these social connections. You might also comment on the value you get from each of them.
   - Do you have a sense that overall the connections on your list make your life richer and happier? _____
   - Is there any area of your social life that you feel you have neglected and would like to rehabilitate or put more effort into and attention on? _____
     _____
   - Is there any part of your social life that is unsatisfying and you would like to change to make it better? _____

3. Let's now assess your sense of optimism.
   - When you face troubles or problems, do you tend to be bleak in your outlook? Hopeful?
   - When there is trouble, do you tend to think things will be better before long, or that this is just another in a long line of troubles?
   - Do you get down on yourself and think there is something wrong with you when you are stressed or face difficulties?
   - Do you tend to see problems as passing things or evidence of more deep-seated and pervasive issues?

We will discuss the optimism/pessimism spectrum in a later chapter, but for now just notice your tendencies. The good news is that if you tend to be pessimistic, this automatic response has been shown to be changeable, and that change can have an impact on your sense of happiness and well-being.

4. Assess your habits of gratitude and appreciation.
   - Do you find yourself regularly feeling grateful? _____
   - Do you frequently express your gratitude to others? _____
   - Do you often "stop to smell the roses," or do you often get caught in the day-to-day and get too busy to notice the everyday wonders and pleasures of life? _____
     _____

5. Do you have a sense that you have found and are living a life with purpose and meaning?
   - Do you have a sense that the work you do is part of why you are alive? _____
     _____
   - Do you have a sense that you are part of something bigger? _____
     _____

- Do you know the reason you are alive? _____

  _____

- Are you fulfilling your purpose? _____

  _____

Okay, that was our quick walk-through and introduction to some of the most cogent issues that impact happiness and well-being. Don't worry about your answers. We weren't trying to get you to judge yourself or decide whether what you are doing or ways you are being are right or wrong. We just wanted to start to raise your awareness of these areas and how they might affect your life and well-being.

Knowing Your Signature Strengths as a Therapist

Overview

One of the cornerstones of Positive Psychology is character or signature strengths. The concept of character strengths evolved out of examining positive youth development and the exploration of what qualities represent "good character." Character in this sense has evolved into a "family of positive dispositions" (Peterson, 2006). In general, character or signature strengths are positive traits that include individual differences such as perspective, curiosity, kindness, gratitude, hope, and teamwork. Researchers Peterson and Seligman (2004) identified 24 character strengths and organized them under the following six core virtues:

Virtue #1: *Strengths of Wisdom and Knowledge*: include positive traits related to the acquisition and use of information in the service of the good life.

  1. Creativity
  2. Curiosity
  3. Love of learning
  4. Open-mindedness
  5. Perspective

Virtue #2: *Strengths of Courage*: entail the exercise of will to accomplish goals in the face of opposition, external or internal.

  6. Authenticity
  7. Bravery
  8. Persistence
  9. Zest

Virtue #3: *Strengths of Humanity*: include positive traits that manifest in caring relationships with others.

  10. Kindness
  11. Love
  12. Social intelligence

Virtue #4: *Strengths of Justice*: are broadly social, relevant to the optimal interaction between the individual and the group or the community.

  13. Fairness
  14. Leadership
  15. Teamwork

Virtue #5: *Strengths of Temperance*: are positive traits that protect us from excess.

  16. Forgiveness/mercy
  17. Modesty/humility
  18. Prudence
  19. Self-regulation

Virtue #6: *Strengths of Transcendence*: strengths that allow individuals to forge connections to the larger universe and thereby provide meaning to their lives.

20. Appreciation of beauty and excellence
21. Gratitude
22. Hope
23. Humor
24. Religiousness/spirituality

The purpose of this exercise is to familiarize you as a therapist with the aforementioned character strengths. With this understanding, you can continue to develop your strengths and better help your clients develop and expand their strengths in the future.

Suggestions for Use

This exercise is for therapists. A parallel exercise, "Knowing Your Character Strengths as a Client," is available for use with clients. To complete this exercise, you will need access to the Internet and the website, www.authentichappiness.org. The Internet portion of this exercise will take approximately 30 minutes to complete. It is also advisable to have a means for saving or printing out your results.

Exercise

To complete this exercise, please complete the following steps.

1. You will need the following resources for this exercise:
   * Access to a computer.
   * An e-mail address.
   * Ability to save your results to the computer or a flash drive for later access. (*Note:* You will be able to save your results on the website you will be accessing; however, you may want to access those results more quickly and at times that you may not be able to connect to the Internet.)
   * Access to a printer if you would prefer a hard copy of your results.
   * Approximately 30 minutes of your time.
2. Connect to the Internet. Next, proceed to www.authentichappiness.org.
3. Create a login.
4. Log in. Select and complete the VIA Signature Strengths Questionnaire.
5. Review the results of your survey. Pay particular attention to your top five strengths. List those strengths in the space below.
   My Top Five Strengths:

   1. _____
   2. _____
   3. _____
   4. _____
   5. _____

6. What stands out for you in reviewing the results from your survey?

_____

_____

_____

_____

7. Next, consider an example of how you use each of your top five strengths in the present. Write those examples in the spaces below.

How I Use My Top Five Strengths in the Present:

1. _____
2. _____
3. _____
4. _____
5. _____

8. Choose one of your top five character strengths. Think of one thing you can do over the next week to develop that strength further. What you choose to do should be different from what you have done in the past or present regarding that strength. Write your plan in the space below.

_____

_____

_____

_____

9. What did you learn as a result of completing this exercise? How can you use what you have learned to help your clients?

_____

_____

_____

_____

References

Peterson, C. (2006). *A primer in positive psychology*. New York: Oxford.

Peterson, C., & Seligman, M. E. P. (2004). *Character strengths and virtues: A handbook and classification*. Washington, DC: American Psychological Association.

Knowing Your Signature Strengths as a Client

Overview

This exercise is the client parallel to "Knowing Your Signature Strengths as a Therapist." The concept of character strengths is a cornerstone of Positive Psychology. The concept of character or signature strengths evolved out of positive youth development and the exploration of what qualities represent "good character." Character in this sense has evolved into a "family of positive dispositions" (Peterson, 2006). In general, character strengths are positive traits that include individual differences such as perspective, curiosity, kindness, gratitude, hope, and teamwork. Researchers Peterson and Seligman (2004) identified 24 character strengths and organized them under the following six core virtues:

Virtue #1: *Strengths of Wisdom and Knowledge*: include positive traits related to the acquisition and use of information in the service of the good life.

1. Creativity
2. Curiosity
3. Love of learning
4. Open-mindedness
5. Perspective

Virtue #2: *Strengths of Courage*: entail the exercise of will to accomplish goals in the face of opposition, external or internal.

6. Authenticity
7. Bravery
8. Persistence
9. Zest

Virtue #3: *Strengths of Humanity*: include positive traits that manifest in caring relationships with others.

10. Kindness
11. Love
12. Social intelligence

Virtue #4: *Strengths of Justice*: are broadly social, and relevant to the optimal interaction between the individual and the group or the community.

13. Fairness
14. Leadership
15. Teamwork

Virtue #5: *Strengths of Temperance*: are positive traits that protect us from excess.

16. Forgiveness/mercy
17. Modesty/humility
18. Prudence
19. Self-regulation

Virtue #6: *Strengths of Transcendence*: those that allow individuals to forge connections to the larger universe and thereby provide meaning to people's lives.

20. Appreciation of beauty and excellence
21. Gratitude
22. Hope
23. Humor
24. Religiousness/spirituality

The purpose of this exercise is twofold: (1) to help your clients identify their character strengths, and (2) to more actively employ character strengths in everyday life.

Suggestions for Use

This is an exercise for clients. It is recommended that therapists complete a parallel exercise, entitled "Knowing Your Signature Strengths as a Therapist," prior to working with clients on this exercise. To complete this exercise, the client will need access to the Internet and the website, www.authentichappiness.org. The Internet portion of this exercise will take approximately 30 minutes to complete. It is also recommended that there be a means for saving or printing out the results. Before having the client complete this exercise, it is recommended that the therapist go over the resources needed for the exercise.

Exercise

The client will need the following resources for this exercise:

• Access to a computer.
• An e-mail address.
• Ability to save his (her) results to the computer or a flash drive for later access. (*Note:* The client will be able to save his (her) results on the website; however, the client may want to access those results more quickly and at times that he (she) may not be able to connect to the Internet.)
• Access to a printer if the client would prefer a hard copy of the results.
• Approximately 30 minutes of time.

Next, have the client complete the following steps.

1. Connect to the Internet. Next, proceed to www.authentichappiness.org.
2. Create a login.
3. Log in. Select and complete the VIA Signature Strengths Questionnaire.
4. For the client: Review the results of your survey. Pay particular attention to your top five character strengths. List your top strengths in the space below.
   My Top Five Strengths:

   1. _____
   2. _____
   3. _____
   4. _____
   5. _____

5. Ask the client: "What stands out for you in reviewing the results from your survey?"

_____

_____

_____

_____

6. Think of an example of how you use each of your top five strengths in the present. Write those examples in the space below.

How I Use My Top Five Strengths in the Present:

1. _____
2. _____
3. _____
4. _____
5. _____

7. Choose one of your top five strengths. Think of one thing you can do over the next week to develop that strength further. What you choose to do should be different from what you have done in the past or present regarding that strength. Write your plan in the space below.

_____

_____

_____

_____

8. What did you learn as a result of completing this exercise? How can you use what you have learned to help your clients?

_____

_____

_____

_____

9. Talk with your therapist about your top strengths and what you learned from this exercise.

References

Peterson, C. (2006). *A primer in positive psychology*. New York: Oxford.

Peterson, C., & Seligman, M. E. P. (2004). *Character strengths and virtues: A handbook and classification*. Washington, DC: American Psychological Association.

Something Different Each Day: Using Signature Strengths in New Ways

Overview

This exercise is designed as a continuation to the client exercise entitled "Knowing Your Signature Strengths as a Client." The purpose of this exercise is to help clients to use their top strengths in new and creative ways in the future. In doing so, clients will be able to use their strengths to experience higher degrees of well-being and to better face future challenges.

Suggestions for Use

It is necessary that clients first complete the exercise entitled "Knowing Your Signature Strengths as a Client."

It is further recommended that therapists complete two exercises entitled "The Four Pillars of Positive Psychology" and "Knowing Your Signature Strengths as a Therapist" prior to working with clients on this exercise. The latter will familiarize therapists with the concept of signature (character) strengths.

Exercise

For this exercise, have the client complete the following steps.

1. List your top signature strengths (from the exercise "Knowing My Signature Strengths as a Client") in the space below.
   My Top Five Strengths:

   1. _____
   2. _____
   3. _____
   4. _____
   5. _____

2. Select one of your top five signature strengths and write it in the space below.

   _____

3. Think of how you can use the signature strength you selected in a different way, each day for the following seven days.

   Examples:

Signature Strength	Action
Open-mindedness	*In conversation, take a position that is at odds with your private opinion.*
Curiosity	*Read about something that you know nothing about.*
Humor	*Make at least one person smile or laugh per day.*
Leadership	*Organize a social get-together with your friends.*
Appreciation of beauty	*At least once a day, stop and notice the natural beauty of something.*

Day 1: _____

_____

Day 2: _____

_____

Day 3: _____

_____

Day 4: _____

_____

Day 5: _____

_____

Day 6: _____

_____

Day 7: _____

_____

Be sure to actively practice your signature strength in the ways listed in the space above!

4. At the end of seven days, reflect on and write what you have learned as a result of this exercise. If possible, discuss what you have learned with your therapist.

_____

_____

_____

_____

5. Repeat Steps 2 and 4, using a different signature strength from your list of top five.
6. Once you have completed this exercise with each of your top five signature strengths, continue with the other strengths listed on your survey.

The Pygmalion Effect

Overview

Some years ago, Robert Rosenthal (Rosenthal & Jacobson, 1992) coined the term the "Pygmalion Effect" to describe the tendency we have to bring our ideas and expectations to life in others (or during social science experiments if they are not double-blind studies). This effect is based on the Greek story of Pygmalion, a sculptor who made a statue of his ideal woman, with which he then fell in love. The gods, so moved by the beauty of his art and his love, brought the statue to life. In a similar way, we tend to bring our expectations and ideas to life in our clients. Executive editor for the online *National Teaching and Learning Forum* James Rhem (1999) writes:

> When teachers expect students to do well and show intellectual growth, they do; when teachers do not have such expectations, performance and growth are not so encouraged and may in fact be discouraged in a variety of ways. (p. 1)

Bill was speaking about this during a presentation he did for a school district. The counselors and teachers there told him a true-life story about the Pygmalion Effect in action. It seems as if a teacher was driven off from the teaching profession by "the class from hell." She just couldn't get them to behave and they regularly disrupted whatever attempts at teaching she tried. When she resigned, no other teacher at the school was willing to take her place, so the principal, in desperation, called a student teacher from the year before who had applied for but was turned down for a teaching position, and offered her the job without telling her about the nature of the class. She accepted and when she showed up for work, he showed her to her classroom and quickly beat a retreat. When he visited the class some weeks later, however, he was surprised to find the class well-behaved and cooperative. After the students left, he congratulated the new teacher on how well the class was doing. She thanked him and then said, "Well, really, thank you, because I discovered your little secret the first day." "You did?" he said uncomfortably. "Yes, the previous teacher had left a clue," she said and pulled open her desk drawer. "I found their IQ scores listed here." The principal looked at the list and saw the students' names with various numbers such as 150, 145, 149, 170, and so on. He was perplexed for a moment, and then it struck him. Those were their locker numbers! The teacher had mistakenly assumed she had very bright students (their locker numbers were grouped together because they were in the same homeroom) and that they just needed a creative approach to engage them in learning. She treated them as capable, and they responded by being capable.

Suggestions for Use

There are two implications of the Pygmalion Effect in applying Positive Psychology in therapy. One is to beware of low or negative expectations of clients. Those expectations may influence the clients and the course of therapy in bad directions. The other obvious implication is to expect the best from your clients—expect them to change in positive directions, to be capable, and to be positively motivated and sincere in their desire to change. Occasionally, students or supervisees will ask us what we do when clients don't really want to change or they are getting hidden gains from having their problems or symptoms. Our reply is that we don't have those thoughts. We come to our therapeutic encounters with a certain mind-set partly due to our therapeutic values (we believe in people and their possibilities) and partly because we know about the Pygmalion Effect.

Exercise

Consider the following ways to use this strategy in sessions:

- Be careful about reading thick files filled with discouraging or negative diagnoses or prognoses before you see the client, the family, or the couple. We usually prefer to see clients before we read those charts to develop our own first impressions rather than having them influenced too much by others with different philosophies and values.
- With cases in which you find yourself being annoyed or frustrated with certain clients, check your expectations and ideas about them. If you can, go to a neutral or more positive mind-set.

References

Rhem, J. (1999). Pygmalion in the classroom. *National Teaching and Learning Forum, 8*(2), 1–4.

Rosenthal, R., & Jacobson, L. (1992). *Pygmalion in the classroom.* New York: Irvington.

The Plus Side

Overview

For the first 100 years, psychology and, subsequently, psychotherapy focused almost exclusively on pathology and deficit. Emphasis was on the amelioration or removal of symptoms; moving people from being sick to not sick, or said differently, from a negative to a neutral state. It was largely believed that people could not go from a negative to a positive state and be healthy. Fortunately there were outliers to this kind of thinking. Carl Jung, Abraham Maslow, Carl Rogers, and others saw a positive side to the human condition. Soon others followed—those who focused not just on the problems people faced, but on helping such persons achieve a higher quality of life. Known as the "plus" side of life, emphasis was placed on how people could develop their resiliencies, coping skills, connections to others, and so on, to live healthier lives and prevent illness. The purpose of this exercise is to help clients move from a zero state to a positive state—to a plus one, plus two, or beyond by building on the four pillars of Positive Psychology discussed throughout this book: Positive Emotion, Meaning, Positive Relationships, and Positive Accomplishments.

Suggestions for Use

Introduce to clients the idea that there are two major focuses of psychotherapy. The first is to help people with the concerns and problems that affect their functioning. The second is to assist people with increasing their life satisfaction and well-being. With the latter, we strive to help people to experience more of the positive side of life, to live happier and healthier lives. Talk with clients about how this exercise can help them build the "plus" side of their lives so that they will not merely experience a reduction in symptoms but that they will flourish in the future. It may also be helpful to explore the benefits of the positive side of life—increased happiness and joy, greater meaning in life, improved relationships, and more accomplishment. These "pluses" can also contribute to better health, longevity, and well-being.

Exercise

For this exercise, say to the client:

> *In addition to working on the concern or problem you are currently facing there is much more that can be done to achieve the life you want for yourself. That is, resolving a problem will likely get you back to "zero," so to speak, but it does not necessarily mean that you will be happier and more satisfied with your life. This exercise will help you to move to the "plus" side of your life so that you may flourish.*

Next, have the client complete each of the sections that follow.

1. Take a moment to consider the kinds of things inspire you, move you, bring about meaning for you, or connect you in positive ways with others throughout your life. Do not limit your thinking to where you live, who you know, or what you do career-wise. Scan the "bigger" world for things that could make your life just a little more satisfying even if you have yet to have specific experiences with those things. In the space provided below, make a list of the things that come to mind. Try to be spontaneous.

_____

_____

_____

_____

_____

_____

_____

_____

_____

2. Next, on a scale of 1 to 5, with 1 representing a low degree of influence the item might have on your overall life satisfaction and 5 representing a very high degree of influence the item might have on your life satisfaction, assign a rating to each of the things you listed under Step 1. Write the assigned number next to each item.

3. Select the top five from your list and write them in the space below. After you have done this, choose one of the items from your list and proceed to Step 4.

1. _____
2. _____
3. _____
4. _____
5. _____

4. Referring to the item you selected in Step 3, describe any positive emotions, meaning, connection to others, or accomplishments that experiencing more of that item might bring about for you.

_____

_____

_____

_____

_____

_____

_____

_____

5. Identify and plan a single step that you can take to experience the item you listed in Step 3 more fully in your life. Make sure the step is something that you can realistically do over the next two days.

6. Take the step described in Step 5.

7. Write any positive emotions, new meanings, new connections, or sense of accomplishment you experienced from taking the step described in Step 5.

8. Make a plan to continue the activity you have engaged in.

9. Add one additional activity from your list (Step 3) and repeat Steps 4 through 8.

Happy Talk, Keep Talking Happy Talk

Overview

A leading Positive Psychology researcher, Barbara Fredrickson, has the "broaden and build" theory of the usefulness of positive emotions. Negative emotions have their use, she thinks. They help narrow your focus. This is important sometimes, like when you are running from some potential danger. Positive emotions, in her view (and backed up by her and others' research), help people broaden their awareness and focus of attention (Fredrickson, 1998). This broadening opens them up to new input and learning, which in turn builds skills and abilities. Several studies support this view and they can be instructive for therapists.

Suggestions for Use

While not avoiding or minimizing problem talk, which is after all what brought most people into treatment, a skilled therapist learns to marble that problem talk with talk about solutions, exceptions to the problem, positive coping skills, resilience, competence, strengths, new perspectives, humor, and other aspects of the situation so that the negative talk doesn't overwhelm or stress the person in treatment too much.

We offer the following case example to assist with this exercise:

Bill was once giving a presentation to home-based family workers. As he discussed a more solution-based way of working, a young woman raised her hand and told him of a family with which she was working recently. The teenager was described by everyone the caseworker had heard from as incorrigible, a sociopath, trouble, uncooperative, etc. She was having some difficulty finding any redeeming qualities of this young man, even from himself. He also described himself as a "bad kid." One day, however, during her daily visit to the family home, the boy fell asleep during the session. The caseworker asked the parents to wake him up, and they suggested he be allowed to sleep. They explained that he had been up all night with his newborn baby sister, comforting her with her bad case of colic. No once else had been able to get the baby to calm down and stop coughing and crying except this "bad boy." The caseworker said that when she heard that story, she knew there was another side to this young man about which she had heard very little. She felt hope for the case for the first time.

Exercise

For the next week or so, practice listening for exceptions, solutions, strengths, competence, positive coping, competence, and resilience.

- When you hear any of these more positive reports or hints, if appropriate, ask more about them. If it is not the right moment to ask about them, take note of them and return to them later.
- If you don't hear any reports of such things, marble in some questions that might elicit such reports in your assessment or session.

Reference

Fredrickson, B. (1998). What good are positive emotions? *Review of General Psychology, 2,* 300–319.

Those Were the Days

Overview

Researchers asked children who were about to perform a new learning task to spend 30 seconds remembering happy things. They found that those children did better on learning tasks they were given just after remembering the happy stuff (Masters, Barden, & Ford, 1979). When clients come to therapy, we are hoping they learn new things (new ways of thinking about and viewing things, new habits and actions, new ways of approaching situations and others). It makes sense, therefore, to spend a short time before asking them to learn something new, to have them evoke a pleasant memory.

Suggestions for Use

This insight from Positive Psychology could be especially useful for clients for whom learning new things is challenging. And we therapists should keep in mind that when we ask our clients, even those who have a relatively easier time learning new things but who might be stressed at the moment, for change. For example, a couple who reaches a crucial point in couples therapy where the tensions are high might be helped by taking a moment to remember a time of connections or happiness before asking them to change their conflict styles.

Virginia Satir, the late family systems therapist and developer of Conjoint Family Therapy, would at times ask couples in the midst of conflict to recount what had first attracted them to one another. When they were sufficiently connected to those positive reminiscences, she would then guide them through making relational changes.

Exercise

For this exercise, focus on the following points with your clients:

- When asking clients to shift their habits or viewpoints, spend a short time reminding them of some pleasant memory they have related that is somehow connected to the challenge they are facing.
- When a client is reacting defensively, ask them to stop and refocus for a moment. Ask them to recall a pleasant vacation or a particularly good time in their lives. Explain that this brief interlude is meant to get them recharged and ready for the next piece of changework they will do.
- You might suggest that clients bring in a photograph of a treasured friend or of themselves at a happy time in their lives and refer to it if the going gets tough in therapy.

Reference

Masters, J., Barden, R., & Ford, M. (1979). Affective states, expressive behavior, and learning in children. *Journal of Personality and Social Psychology, 37,* 380–390.

Evoking a Positive Mood

Overview

Another study, akin to the previous one about recalling pleasant moments, showed that interns were better at diagnosing a hard-to-diagnose case of liver disease after they had been given a piece of candy (Isen, Rosensweig, & Young, 1991). They didn't eat the candy (so a surge in blood sugar wasn't a factor), but just having received a very small gift, they were in a more pleasant (recall Barbara Fredrickson's "broaden and build" theory of the utility of positive emotions) and more open state. Because we as therapists are hoping to invite our clients to be more open, evoking a positive mood might help the change process.

Suggestions for Use

This exercise is designed for use with clients, but of course, if you have a particularly problematic client in mind, you could use any of the activities to help you develop a more open mind-set.

Exercise

For this exercise, consider doing one or more of the following things to influence and encourage more "positivity" among your clients:

- Leave little pieces of candy in your waiting room.
- Leave joke books in the waiting room.
- Put a beautiful video on a TV in the waiting room.
- Give clients small, unexpected treats, such as a handout for coping with the holidays if they have had trouble in that area previously, right before the session. These little gifts can help clients get in a more positive frame of mind and mood.

Reference

Isen, A., Rosensweig, A., & Young, M. (1991). The influence of positive affect on clinical problem solving. *Medical Decision Making, 11,* 221–227.

Last Impressions

Overview

It turns out that the last thing we experience influences what we remember. Researchers were searching for a way to increase the percentage of people at risk for colon cancer to return for recommended follow-up visits after their first colonoscopy. This was in the days when colonoscopies were painful (these days, physicians tend to put patients in "twilight states" to make the procedure much less uncomfortable). Many patients, after the rather painful first procedure, would tend to avoid future procedures. But either because they had family risk factors or the first exam had shown they were at risk for cancer, they were urged to schedule follow-up colonoscopies. Researchers discovered a clever way to increase compliance. Because they knew from other experiments that people tended to judge experiences by what they remember about them and that the last thing that happens in an experience tends to color the memory of the whole experience, they asked the examining physicians to try leaving the proctoscope in at the end of the procedure for a few minutes without moving it around. This resulted in a significant increase in those patients scheduling follow-up procedures (Redelmeier & Kahneman, 1996).

Suggestions for Use

Be sure to end therapy on a positive note (or at the very least, a neutral one). If the client has been upset, angry, or in some negative mood during the session, help him shift his mood or attention before he leaves. The easiest way to do this is to end the session with a compliment.

Exercise

Write a list of compliments and acknowledgments you could give clients to end the session on a positive note:

- It might be about the effort they made to come to the session. Some people have to rearrange schedules, deal with difficult insurance matters, take public transportation, and so on. Some people have had to overcome reluctance or fear of the therapy process, medications, or something else about the therapy process. You can let them know you are aware of and appreciate the effort it took them to come in.
- It could be about the progress they made during the session or over the course of treatment.
- It could be about a particular insight or piece of therapeutic work they did in the session.
- It could be about some challenging thing they faced between sessions.

Reference

Redelmeier, D., & Kahneman, D. (1996). Patients' memories of painful medical treatments: Real-time and retrospective evaluations of two minimally invasive procedures. *Pain, 116,* 3–8.

Labels Can Stick Like Crazy Glue

Overview

Attribution Theory tells us that the meanings and labels we attribute to situations, things, or people strongly influence our subsequent behavior and perceptions. So we can make an effort to attribute good labels and avoid unhelpful labels in therapy.

Researchers told some schoolchildren that they seemed like the kind of students who "care about good handwriting." Those kids subsequently spent more of their free time practicing handwriting, even when they thought no one was watching them (Cialdini, Eisenberg, Green, Rhoads, & Bator, 1998).

In another experiment, students in a graduate-level class were asked to evaluate a potential new faculty member after he taught a sample class for them. Unbeknown to the students, half of them were given a biographical sketch of the potential faculty member that had two small words different from what the other half were given. We have provided the biographical statements below with the different words highlighted in bold.

> Mr. _____ is a graduate student in the Department of Economics and Social Science here at MIT. He has had three semesters of teaching experience in psychology at another college. This is his first semester teaching EC 70. He is 26 years old, a veteran, and married. People who know him consider him to be a **very warm** person, industrious, critical, practical, and determined.

> Mr. _____ is a graduate student in the Department of Economics and Social Science here at MIT. He has had three semesters of teaching experience in psychology at another college. This is his first semester teaching EC 70. He is 26 years old, a veteran, and married. People who know him consider him to be a **rather cold** person, industrious, critical, practical, and determined.

The class got the same lecture, but at the end, when asked to rate the instructor for possible hiring as an instructor, the students who had read the description of a **"very warm"** person rated him as *"good-natured, considerate of others, informal, sociable, popular, humorous, and humane,"* while those who read that he was **"rather cold"** rated him as *"self-centered, formal, unsociable, unpopular, irritable, humorless, and ruthless."*

The point these experiments make to therapists in a clinical setting is that the labels and attributions we have been provided or come up with based on our theories and backgrounds can influence both the evaluations we make of the clients and their possibilities and perhaps even the sense the clients have of these things.

This doesn't mean we have to avoid any diagnostic labels (they are useful for insurance reimbursement, if for nothing else), but we must be careful about using labels that are discouraging, blaming, attribute bad intentions, or imply that people can't or won't change.

In a recent study, Carol Dweck and colleagues (Blackwell, Trzesniewski, & Dweck, 2007) found that people who believe personality can change were more likely than others to bring up concerns and deal with problems in a constructive way. Dweck et al. hold the view that a fixed mind-set can foster a categorical, all-or-nothing view of people's qualities; this view tends to lead to ignoring festering problems or, at the other extreme, giving up on a relationship at the first sign of trouble.

A friend of Bill's told him a story about going to a consultation group at a new job he took at a mental health facility. In his first meeting, he noticed that sometimes, when someone in the group was discussing a case, the psychologist consultant would silently hold up two fingers and the discussion would halt and move to a different client. After the meeting, Bill's friend asked one of his fellow employees what the two fingers meant and why the discussion would stop when the consultant held them up. "He means that the patient is Axis 2, and because they have a personality disorder and one can't change personality, we shouldn't even bother to discuss them." Bill's friend, being more oriented toward a solution-based and hopeful approach to therapy, was stunned by this explanation. And so are we. If you attribute things to your client (or patient if you prefer) that preclude the possibility for change, that, in our view, is not a statement about reality, but an attribution. Find another attribution that can fit with the facts as well as the previous unhelpful attribution that gives you and the client some hope for better things to come.

Suggestions for Use

These are the attributions to be careful to avoid from you as a therapist or from clients and their families or the people who might influence them:

- Ideas of incompetence
- Ideas of unwillingness to change
- Ideas of inability to change
- Ideas of bad intentions
- Ideas of bad or deficient personality traits
- Ideas of impossibility

When you as a therapist come across such ideas in yourself or in others related to your client or the course of therapy, gently challenge them and offer alternate ideas.

If the idea is one you've developed or gotten stuck on, consider checking with colleagues or a supervisor to get different perspectives or ideas about the person or situation. Or try reading a book or attending a workshop with someone who has a different and more hopeful view about clients or about this type of client.

If the idea comes from the person or their intimates, you might say something like: "That might be the way it is. Have you considered this other way of thinking about it?" Or, "Maybe he can't change or maybe he hasn't been approached in a way that engages his motivation to change yet."

Exercise

For this exercise, reflect on the following points and consider what you might do in response to them.

- Think of a very challenging case you've dealt with in the past. Identify the unhelpful and unhopeful attributions you might have made in this case. Then consider a different way of thinking about the person, people, or situation. What might be a more generous, helpful, or hopeful attribution to make that would still fit with the facts of the situation?
- Identify a label that a current client has and consider a different label for the same trait or situation. For example, rather than "resistant," the person could be seen as "hesitant," or "frightened," or "skeptical," or "confused," or "coerced." Or, instead of being "unable to express his feelings," one could imagine the person has "learned not to notice and articulate very easily what is happening with them." Instead of being borderline, perhaps the person could be re-seen as "ambivalent." We don't suggest an unrealistically positive view here, but a more generous, change-oriented one.
- For the next few weeks, seek to discover anything or any area in the client's life that can and does change rather than orienting to the aspects of them and their lives that don't change or aren't changing.

References

Blackwell, L., Trzesniewski, K., & Dweck, C. (2007). Implicit theories of intelligence predict achievement across an adolescent transition: A longitudinal study and an intervention. *Child Development, 78*(1), 246–263.

Cialdini, R., Eisenberg, N., Green, B., Rhoads, K., & Bator, R. (1998). Undermining the undermining effect of reward on sustained interest. *Journal of Applied Social Psychology, 28,* 249–263.

Kelley, H. (1950). The warm-cold variable in first impressions of persons. *Journal of Personality, 18,* 431–439.

Attention! Deficit Disorder: Finding Contexts of Competence

Overview

When people come to therapy, they are often feeling incompetent and resourceless. But those same clients usually have areas in which they are quite competent and feel confident. Helping them connect with this sense of competence can shift them into a more resourceful state as well as sometimes provide real skills and solutions to the problem at hand.

For example, a wife was frustrated with her engineer husband because he was not good at expressing affection. She was on the verge of seeking a divorce because she had complained about this for quite some time—to no avail. In therapy, the husband was asked about what he liked so much about being an engineer. He said he liked to map out and analyze problems so he could help solve them. It was then suggested he make an analysis of the problems in his marriage and bring it next time. He showed up with a detailed diagram and happily showed it to the therapist and his wife. It turned out according to his analysis that there was a "glitch" in the system when he first arrived home from work most days. Some discussions clarified that he would usually go upstairs without, or with only barely, greeting his wife, who found this hurtful.

When we brainstormed solutions, we came up with the "patch" that he could seek out and hug his wife when he walked in the door. He did so, but she said most of the time the hug was perfunctory and not satisfying to her. We them created some "specs" for the husband, detailing what a "good hug" consisted of, according to her standards. It was 45 seconds, full frontal contact. That was minimum specs. Maximum was that he would wait for her to break off the hug first. He readily dove into mastering good hugs and the wife was not only happier with the hugs, but was even more impressed with his obvious energy and enthusiasm for solving their problems. She saw that he had energy to change their marriage and gave up her plans for divorce.

Suggestions for Use

Investigate any areas of competence the client might have, asking him (her) and anyone else who might have such knowledge. Explore

- Hobbies/interests
- Work skills or knowledge
- Social skills or abilities
- Artistic or creative skills or abilities

Another way that you might use this strategy is to ask people about the wisest, kindest, most supportive person they know and what that person might do or suggest in the problem situation. This often evokes wisdom and competence from clients.

Exercise

For this exercise, focus on the following areas with your clients:

- Find out in what settings the person is competent and skilled.
- Ask them in more detail about this area and how they would handle difficult moments in that setting or context.
- Suggest that the person transfer skills, knowledge, and abilities from a context of competence to the problem area.

- Find out who the person knows and knew who was uncommonly wise, kind, or supportive or who believes or believed in the person and their goodness and abilities.
- What advice would that kind, supportive person give them or others who were facing this or a similar problem?

Questions to Use

- What do you do well or know a lot about? Where do you feel confident or competent?
- How might you use this competence or knowledge to help solve or cope with this problem?

Additional Resource

O'Hanlon, B., & Wilk, J. (1987). *Shifting contexts: The generation of effective psychotherapy.* New York: Guilford.

Symptom Trance: Waking Yourself and the Client

Overview

Psychologist Stephen Gilligan has a funny way of talking about clients with whom we have become stuck. He describes a trance induction process that can go like this:

> (Client looks at therapist): *Hello, I am glad to meet you. I'm depression. When you look at me, you will see only depression. I have always been depression; I'll always be depression. When you look at me, you will no longer see a person; you will see only depression and hopelessness. Go deeper and deeper into the depression trance. Deeper and deeper.*

When this happens, the therapist has been invited into a narrowed, symptom-focused trance. The client is already in such a state, but some have become so skilled at inviting others into this state that one can become convinced they will never change.

We refer to this a "symptom trance," in which the person becomes so absorbed in this resourceless state that they find it difficult to come out of the trance. If the therapist also becomes induced into this state, he (she) may find himself (herself) thinking things such as the following:

> Perhaps this person can't change. If I had such a life, suicide wouldn't be that bad an option.
> Oh, no, this client is on my appointment book again.

In our view, then, it is imperative for therapists to learn how to recognize and come out of the symptom trance.

First, learn to recognize when you (or the client) are in a symptom trance. Of course, one sign is if not much is changing in the therapy process. Another is if you as the therapist find yourself getting discouraged and hopeless in the therapy process. Another is if most people involved with the client and the case have the same story or idea about him (her) or it. Another is if the client continues to do, think, or feel the same kinds of things over and over without much variation.

In our view, there are healing trances and problematic (or symptom) trances. A healing trance validates the person, connects them with resources, and opens up possibilities. A problematic trance invalidates the person, disconnects them from resources, and closes down possibilities.

Suggestions for Use

One hint about what to do when confronted with a symptom trance in you or the client is indicated by the following story:

A physician who didn't quite complete his medical training found himself on the battlefield in France in World War II, next to a French soldier who had been severely wounded in battle. His intestines were split open and threatened to spill out onto the ground, quickly ending the soldier's life. The physician knew that if he could get the man to remain still, he might be able to save his life; but try as he might, with his little French, he could not communicate this to the writhing soldier next to him. In desperation, he found himself remembering a demonstration of hypnosis he had seen during his medical studies. Emulating all he could remember and using what little French he had, he repeated in a soft voice, "Your eyes are closing, your eyes are closing." After a number of repetitions of this phrase, to his relief and amazement, the French soldier stopped writhing and seemed to go into a trance. His life was saved.

When he recounted what he had done to the surgeons, a mixture of British and French doctors, they all began to laugh and explained to him that what he had actually been repeating had been,

"Your ears are closing, your ears are closing." What we found interesting about the story is what it reveals about trance induction. The words don't matter as much as the repetition of things.

And this leads to our clue about how to break up the symptom trance and wake up yourself and clients from it. Begin to disrupt repetitive patterns in the clients' and your behavior. If they recite a litany of similar complaints and reports to you week after week, politely but firmly interrupt and ask them about something entirely new and different. If you find yourself drifting away into an unhelpful trance, get up and move around to rouse yourself. Get a glass of water; change pens…whatever you need to do to wake up.

Another clue is that clients who feel invalidated (blamed, shamed, or undermined in their perceptions or sense of things) can go into such symptomatic trances. So, another way to bring them out of a trance is to identify where such shame, blame, or undermining of confidence in their own perceptions and sense of things is occurring and provide some simple validation or relief from blame or shame.

Exercise

For this exercise, focus on one or more the following areas with your clients:

• Notice which clients are inviting you into symptom and unhelpful trances.
• Notice which clients are in such symptom trances.
• Find any repetition in the client's behavior, language, or nonverbals.
• Come up with and implement a plan to disrupt the pattern (and thus the trance) sometime during the session.
• Notice what worked. If nothing did, alter the plan and give it another try.
• If nothing is working, try identifying some place in which the client feels blamed, shamed, or undermined in their sense of things and perceptions. Provide some simple validation or relief from blame or shame. This does not mean that one has to agree with delusional realities or let people off from personal accountability; only that the therapist can stretch to find a way to validate without necessarily agreeing.

Then, write your reactions to trying one or more of the ideas listed. Consider: How did it work? What worked best? What might you do differently in the future as a result of what you have learned?

_____
_____
_____
_____
_____
_____

Additional Resources

Araoz, D. (1984). *The new hypnosis.* New York: Brunner/Mazel [Routledge].
Beahrs, J. (1982). *Unity and multiplicity.* New York: Brunner/Mazel [Routledge].
Gilligan, S. (1987). *Therapeutic trances: The cooperation principle in Ericksonian hypnotherapy.* New York: Brunner/Mazel [Routledge].
Ritterman, M. (1983). *Using hypnosis in family therapy.* San Francisco: Jossey-Bass.
Wolinsky, S. (1991). *Trances people live: Healing approaches in quantum psychology.* Falls Village, CT: The Bramble Company.

Purpose and Meaning

We begin the P.O.S.I.T.I.V.E. framework with purpose and meaning because in many ways these aspects underlie all happiness and well-being. The late psychiatrist and holocaust survivor Viktor Frankl liked to repeat: "You can survive any what if you have a *why*."

In this chapter we provide a number of activities and exercises that will help people explore and develop a sense of meaning and purpose. Cognitive scientist and philosopher Daniel Dennett once asked, rhetorically, "Do you want to know the secret to happiness?" And then proceeded to answer: "Find something more important than yourself and dedicate your life to it."

Playwright George Bernard Shaw has one of his characters utter this profound sentiment:

> This is the true joy in life, the being used up for a purpose recognized by yourself as a mighty one; the being a force of nature instead of a feverish, selfish little clod of ailments and grievances, complaining that the world will not devote itself to making you happy. I am of the opinion that my life belongs to the community, and as long as I live, it is my privilege to do for it whatever I can. I want to be thoroughly used up when I die, for the harder I work the more I live. I rejoice in life for its own sake. Life is no "brief candle" to me. It is a sort of splendid torch which I have got hold of for a moment, and I want to make it burn as brightly as possible before handing it on to future generations. —Bernard Shaw, 1946

And that sentiment captures the essence of this aspect of Positive Psychology, to find a meaning and purpose bigger than oneself; something that makes life worth living.

We discuss personal meaning as well as the notion of "positive institutions." We show how one can take the hurts and frustrations of life and turn them into pathways to meaning and life direction. Traditionally the purview of religion, we can draw on secular traditions as well to mine this rich area of life.

Reference

Bernard Shaw, G. (1946). *Man and superman*. Act III, Don Juan in Hell. London: Penguin Books.

A Connection to Something Bigger

Overview

We tend to exist largely within invisible, psychological boundaries that we have set for ourselves. There is nothing wrong with staying within our comfort zones; however, doing so can restrict our experience with the world. The exercise is to gently push the outer edges of the boundaries we have set to experience greater meaning in life. This exercise is also about connecting with larger experiences in ways that have purpose. In other words, we want to do things not merely for the sake of doing them but to contribute to something bigger than ourselves.

Suggestions for Use

This exercise is for all persons—clients and therapists. In fact, as a therapist you may want to try the exercise before recommending it to a client (by the way, we recommend this with every exercise in this volume). This exercise is akin to the idea of "The Bucket List," a list of those things people intend to do before they pass away. A difference is that the client list created in this exercise is meant to also connect people to things larger than themselves. In doing this exercise, it is recommended that clients identify things that are attainable within an agreed-upon time frame (i.e., six months, two years, etc.). One of the potential benefits of an exercise such as this is that it keeps clients engaged in activities that influence well-being, happiness, meaning and purpose, connection to others, and accomplishment—each of which represent important aspects of Positive Psychology. We advise that therapists talk with clients about the commitment necessary to see this exercise through. If a client is apprehensive, it may be best to try other exercises until the client is ready to embark on this kind of journey.

Exercise

This exercise involves steadfast commitment. Without the commitment to follow through with the process you are about to embark on, it is unlikely you will experience the full benefit. When you are ready, proceed to and follow the steps outlined below.

1. Begin by thinking of the things that you have not yet accomplished in your life but want to be sure to do before your physical time on Earth comes to an end. These can be places you want to go, people you would like to meet, activities you want to try, something new you want to learn, and so on. Don't be concerned about how you will accomplish the things on your list. There's a whole wide world out there, so just imagine! Be sure to write what you imagine in the space below. Try to come up with 8 to 10 items. They do not have to be in any particular order.

   * _____
   * _____
   * _____
   * _____
   * _____
   * _____
   * _____
   * _____
   * _____
   * _____

2. For the next part, review the four areas or "pillars" of Positive Psychology described below. You don't need to know every term. Try to gain a sense of what each pillar stands for. Ask your therapist for help if needed.

    Pillar #1: *Positive emotion:* subjective well-being, happiness, gratitude, savoring, flow, signature strengths, possibilities.

    Pillar #2: *Meaning*: positive institutions, virtues, contribution, service, altruism, hope, future-mindedness, positive deviance.

    Pillar #3: *Positive relationships:* social connections; intimate relationships; positive interactions; pets; church/spiritual communities; professional, work, or interest groups; teams; military units; support groups.

    Pillar #4: *Positive accomplishments:* mastery, competence, achievement, successes, new skills acquisition.

    Now refer back to the list you created in Step 1. Next to each of the things you listed, assign a number that represents the pillar that best matches that item. You may list more than one pillar next to an item.

3. Next, select one item from your list. Transfer that item to the space below.

    _____

    Next, write about how the thing you chose will positively influence your life. One way to do this is by expanding on the pillar you assigned the item.

    _____

    _____

    _____

    _____

4. Think about how you might accomplish the item on your list *and* at the same time contribute to another person's life, your community, a population in need, society at large, or some social issue that marginalizes, restricts, or disempowers people. Please be sure to give this more than just a moment's thought. Write in the space below how you hope to influence the "world beyond" through your activity.

    _____

    _____

    _____

    _____

    _____

    _____

5. Now consider what it will take to actively pursue the item you have selected and explored in this exercise. In the space below, list the steps you will take to make your pursuit a reality.

    1. _____

    2. _____

    3. _____

4. _____

5. _____

6. If possible, talk with your therapist about your plan. Also, report back on the results of your efforts. Consider one or more of the following questions:
   • What happened?
   • What did you notice that is different about yourself?
   • What positive emotions did you experience?
   • What new meanings have you acquired?
   • What difference did your actions make for others? The community? Society?

   _____
   _____
   _____
   _____
   _____
   _____

7. As soon as you can, return to the original list you generated in Step 1 and repeat the steps that follow. Be sure to note the differences that the activities make in your life and in others' lives.

Follow Your Bliss

Overview

Some years ago, in the famous interview Bill Moyers did with mythologist Joseph Campbell, Moyers asked Campbell, "If a student came to you for advice about their life and career direction, what would you say?" Campbell answered without hesitation, "I would tell them: Follow your bliss. If you follow your bliss, you put yourself on a kind of track that has been there all the while, waiting for you, and the life that you ought to be living is the one you are living. Wherever you are—if you are following your bliss, you are enjoying that refreshment, that life within you, all the time."

One way to find meaning and purpose in life is to discover one's bliss. By this, we don't mean what feels good in the moment. We mean more finding what is deeply and meaningfully satisfying or enlivening. Howard Thurman says: "Don't ask yourself what the world needs. Ask yourself what makes you come alive, and go do that, because what the world needs is people who have come alive." We will respectfully disagree that one shouldn't ask oneself what the world needs, but we do agree that a good place to start is with what brings you alive. Without that basic energy, it would be hard to do much good work in the world. Depression or low energy makes it harder to contribute to others.

One of Bill O'Hanlon's favorite stories is one he heard about Charles Darwin. Darwin loved nature and had a large bug collection so he could study all the varieties. One day, while walking several miles from home, the young Darwin came across three large beetles of a type he had never before encountered. He desperately wanted them for his collection, but realized that, with only two hands, he could only bring two back with him. He decided to pop one in his mouth and ran the whole way home with it squiggling in there. (Perhaps that's why we majored in psychology rather than biology. Creepy!) His bliss overcame his aversion to the bug in his mouth.

Another vivid example of following one's bliss comes from the poet Pablo Neruda. His family had him on track to be a civil servant in his native Chile. It would have been a fine life, very secure, with a steady job and good retirement. But fate had different things in mind for the young Pablo. One day, while walking home alone after a football game, a poem came to him unbidden. He was so astonished and moved by this experience that he announced to his disappointed parents that he would no longer pursue the civil service, but was dedicating his life to poetry. He later wrote a poem about his pivotal moment, in which something started in his soul, "fever or forgotten wings; … suddenly I saw the heavens unfastened and open. … I wheeled with the stars. My heart broke loose on the wind." This vivid description gives a sense of what bliss might feel like.

Suggestions for Use

As it did for Pablo Neruda, it often takes some courage to recognize and follow one's bliss. We can serve our clients by helping them in that process. They have often eschewed this path because it seems impractical or they haven't trusted their inner knowledge. If they can follow this blissful energy, they are often closer to finding some deep meaning and purpose in their lives.

Now, some clients do not have a clue about their bliss and will not find their energy or life purpose through this path. That is okay. In the next few sections we provide some other paths to finding meaning and purpose. But because this is a common method for finding life direction and purpose, it's a good place to start.

Exercise

Have clients list activities in the past that have created a great deal of inner satisfaction and joy. Ask them if they have followed that sense of satisfaction and joy in developing that area or activity as a more serious endeavor and, if not, what stopped them. Investigate whether pursuing activities that give this sense of aliveness would be appropriate or meaningful to them at this time in their lives.

Questions to Ask

At appropriate times, with clients who don't have a sense of meaning and purpose, investigate their bliss energy and areas by asking questions such as the following:

- What brings you alive?
- What are you passionate about?
- What makes your soul and heart sing?
- What do you find yourself returning to again and again in your leisure time?
- With what are you soulfully obsessed?

Additional Resource

Campbell, J. (2004). *Pathways to bliss: Mythology and personal transformation.* New York: New World Library.

Follow Your Blisters

Overview

After the phrase "Follow your bliss" had become part of the lexicon, Campbell became concerned that people had misunderstood it to mean he was encouraging hedonism. Campbell is reported to have grumbled, "I should have said, 'Follow your *blisters*.'" Many of your clients are not exactly feeling blissful when they arrive for therapy, so perhaps a more productive direction for investigation is to discover what wounds and hurts they have that might be transformed into life meaning. Instead of bliss, perhaps helping clients get in touch with and use the energy from where they have been "dissed," as young people say these days, to find meaning, purpose, and direction in life would be a better course. (Dissed is short for disrespected.) Where has the client or someone whom they care about been disrespected, that is, hurt, marginalized, put down, wounded, or cursed?

Bill had a colleague at one mental health center at which he worked who told him that when she was in high school, her guidance counselor told her not to bother applying to college because she wasn't smart enough. This wounded her deeply. She became determined to prove him wrong. When she graduated with her bachelor's degree, she sent him a short note: *I guess you were wrong about me.* When she got her master's degree, she sent another little note. When she finished her Ph.D., she let him know about that as well. And when her first book came out, she sent him an autographed copy. Then she stopped writing. She had apparently made her point by then!

But here is what is more poignant and relevant. Her dissertation and first book were about helping adolescents find their way by encouraging them. And that is the point of finding life direction from one's wounds, hurts, disappointments, and so on. If one lets those life experiences sensitize one to that area of suffering and then use that sensitivity to make a life or career direction of changing that for others, one can make meaning and purpose from pain. This is key: One can't express this hurt in destructive ways (e.g., cutting oneself; showing up at work or school with an AK-47 to take revenge on those who dissed you), but must instead make a positive contribution to making things better in this area.

Psychologist Sam Keen writes about this process:

> We all leave childhood with wounds. In time we may transform our liabilities into gifts. The faults that pockmark the psyche may become the source of a man or a woman's beauty. The injuries we have suffered invite us to assume the most human of all vocations—to heal ourselves and others. (from Gurian, 1996)

Suggestions for Use

Investigating clients' wounds and dissatisfactions doesn't have to lead to a sense of victimization or helplessness. We can help clients use this energy to find meaning, purpose, and direction in life.

Exercise

Ask your client some of these questions to discover whether he (she) can mine the value of problems to transform them into meaningful life directions:

- Where have you been wounded?
- Where or about what have you been cursed?
- Where have you or someone you care about been disrespected or treated unfairly?
- How have these experiences sensitized you to the problems or suffering in this area?

- What do you think you might be able to do to relieve or prevent similar suffering for others in the future?
- How could you turn this wound, curse, or disrespect into a blessing, a vocation, a calling, or a life or career direction?

Story to Tell

We heard the following story that might help clients find a way to transform their hurtful experiences into meaningful contributions.

> A tourist in Israel went on a tour bus to visit various locales. The tour guide showed the tourists the Dead Sea. He told them it was dead because it was fed by a river full of minerals that built up, as they had no outlet, and killed all living things in the sea. A while later, they visited the Sea of Galilee and the guide told them that this sea was also fed by a similar river full of minerals with the potential to kill everything, but it was very much alive. The difference: Galilee had an outlet for the water to move through it. The guide said, with a twinkle in his eyes, 'Perhaps this is the secret of life. We must always give away that which is given to us, or else we die inside.'

Reference

Gurian, M. (1996). *The wonder of boys*. New York: Tracher/Penguin.

Additional Resource

O'Hanlon, B. (2009). *A lazy man's guide to success*. Santa Fe, NM: PossibilitE-books.

Follow Your Pissed: Transforming Anger into Life Contribution, Direction, and Meaning

Overview

Sometimes our clients aren't just wounded, they are angry. One of the other energies that can be transformed to create a life direction or meaning is being pissed off. Anger scares people. Even therapists. They want to dampen or get rid of it. But anger can be quite useful and can contribute to a positive life direction and contribution.

Bill became a writer and workshop presenter because he was angry about some of the disrespect and discouraging, negative approaches he saw in the therapy field. He vowed to change his chosen field by introducing more constructive, solution-oriented approaches to change and to insist on respecting clients exactly as they present. That led him to write 30-plus books and travel around the world teaching workshops to introduce these ideas and methods.

The field of Positive Psychology was founded because Martin Seligman was upset when he discovered that most of the research done in psychology had to do with negative states and qualities of people.

Instead of bliss, perhaps helping clients get in touch with and use the energy from where they have been "dissed," as young people say these days, to find meaning, purpose, and direction in life would be a better course. Dissed is short for "disrespected." Where has the client or someone whom they care about been disrespected, that is, hurt, marginalized, put down, wounded, or cursed? Martin Luther King, Jr., said, "Our lives begin to end the day we become silent about things that matter."

Entrepreneur Richard Branson (2006) relates how being angry about what was happening in school got him started and carried him through the difficult days of starting his first business, a magazine for students.

> I started *Student* when I was 15 years old and still at Stowe, the boarding school I went to. I didn't do it to make money—I did it because I wanted to edit a magazine. I didn't like the way I was being taught at school or what was going on in the world and I wanted to put it right. …When I told friends and acquaintances that I intended to produce a proper magazine for sale on a professional, commercial scale, and asked for advice and journalistic contributions, I was confronted with some degree of skepticism and even hoots of laughter. They treated my project like just another schoolboy enthusiasm. One or two shrugged and said I was too young and had no experience. But I was serious—I really believed in myself, believed it could be done and wanted to prove them wrong. I've always been stubborn and, if anything, their negativity strengthened my resolve and made me all the more determined. (Branson, 2006, pp. 6–7)

Remember the key here to transforming anger into meaning: One can't express this anger in destructive ways, but must make a positive contribution to making things better in the area about which one is upset.

Suggestions for Use

We are suggesting that you take clients' anger seriously. You do not have to dissipate it or get them to think more rationally. It can be a powerful signal as to what they can do with their lives that might be meaningful.

Exercise

Ask your client some of these questions to discover whether they can mine the value of anger to transform it into meaningful life directions.

- What upsets you or gets you to want to take action to change or correct or prevent?
- What would you talk about if given an hour of prime time television to influence the nation or the world?
- What injustice do you see happening in the world that you can't sit still for?
- What pisses you off that you would like to change so that it never happens to anyone again?
- How have these experiences sensitized you to the problems or suffering in this area?
- What do you think you might be able to do to relieve or prevent similar suffering for others in the future?
- How could you turn this anger into a vocation, a calling, or a life or career direction?

Reference

Branson, R. (2006). *Screw it, let's do it: Lessons in life*. New York: Random House.

Additional Resource

O'Hanlon, B. (2009). *A lazy man's guide to success*. Santa Fe, NM: PossibilitE-books.

Out of the Box: Getting a Broader Perspective

Overview

Psychologist Warren Berland (1998) has created a method of distilling years of spiritual study into a very brief form. He contends that everyone has the possibility of rapidly attaining a broader perspective on troubles, thus getting them from a narrow, stuck, "in-the-box" experience so common to problems to that broader, "out-of-the-box" perspective.

It is akin to having the "worm's-eye view" of situations, a view in which you are very focused on the moment and the problem, and the "bird's-eye view" in which you can get some broader emotional and time perspective and view things as part of a larger context.

Suggestions for Use

This method may not provide a solution to the problem (and sometimes it does), but it often helps clients get unstuck from their fears or sense of helplessness. And although it is derived from a spiritual base, there is no need to reference spirituality or religion when using this method.

Exercise 1

First, try this method yourself (therapist) to get a sense of how it works.

Step 1 Find a problem to focus upon. Choose something about which you feel stuck, upset, overwhelmed, helpless, powerless, or hopeless. It's best if it is some recurring situation; that is, something you have come up against more than once.

Step 2 Close your eyes and, as much as possible, get a felt sense and vivid memory of what dealing with that problem is like. You might put yourself back in the situation or remember a particular incident in which the problem occurred. Spend a few minutes really getting into the experience.

Step 3 Now put that problem to the side. When you've done that, find a more positive, empowering experience. Remember a time when you felt free, or powerful, or whole, or happy, or in love, or expansive, or holy, or healthy. This could be evoked by a particular incident or by a time or phase in your life. Again, take some time to develop a really good felt, experiential sense of that time or state.

Step 4 Keeping that felt sense present, revisit or reexamine the problem situation. What do you notice from this different perspective? Are there things to do about the problem that didn't seem available before? Is the problem gone from this new perspective? Is it smaller or more distant?

Is the mood or hopefulness of dealing with the problem any different? If so, how? Notice anything else that has shifted.

Exercise 2

Now try the same exercise with clients. When you notice they are feeling stuck or hopeless, spend just a few minutes doing Steps 3 and 4 with them (they are already in touch with the felt sense of the problem, so you can skip the first two steps). After they have done that, ask them the questions listed in Step 4 above.

If they have experienced a significant shift, explore how they might either use the exercise on their own if and when they felt stuck in the future or how they might keep this perspective or some of the possibilities or insights that emerged from the process going in the future.

Reference

Berland, W. (1998). *Out of the box for life.* New York: Harper Collins.

Post-Traumatic Success: The Three Cs

Overview

It was important that we learned to recognize and validate the haunting after-effects of trauma (called Post-Traumatic Stress Disorder in diagnostic parlance). For years, it went unrecognized and people either suffered in silence, thought they were going insane or were weak, or thought they had weak moral fiber. We now know that there are fairly predictable patterns of post-traumatic response although, of course, there are always individual variations.

What has gotten short shrift in the increased recognition and concern about post-traumatic stress is the other side of the coin, post-traumatic success. That is, there is a wealth of data showing that some people derive positive benefits from going through crises and traumas.

A wide range of positive life changes have been reported in many studies of positive effects from tragedies such as heart attack, cancer, fire, death of loved ones, chronic illness, rape, and natural disasters. Those that have been documented are enhanced closeness with others, including loved ones and neighbors; renewed commitment to or changed life priorities; enhanced sense of self-effectiveness; enhanced sensitivity to and empathy for others; and increased knowledge about the negative event experienced. In one study, heart attack survivors were less likely to have had another heart attack and more likely to be in good health eight years post-attack if they had perceived benefit a few weeks following the attack (Affleck, Tennen, Croog, & Levine, 1987).

Some benefits from crisis and trauma shown by the research include

- Enhanced closeness to others
- Renewed commitment to life priorities
- Changed priorities
- Increased sensitivity and empathy for others
- Increased health knowledge
- Increased sense of spirituality
- Enhanced sense of one's effectiveness and ability to do something about one's life
- Greater concern about world issues

Of course, much of the time, there are both negative and positive things that occur for people following trauma. But we have the chance to tip the balance a bit by both increasing awareness of the possibility of having benefits and by encouraging people to do the things that resilient people do after trauma.

Suggestions for Use

A summary of the available research indicates that there are three things than can make the difference between post-traumatic stress and post-traumatic success. These are *Connection, Compassion,* and *Contribution* (O'Hanlon, 2004).

If, as a result of a crisis or trauma, one can become more connected to oneself, others, and something bigger than oneself and others, it is likely to tip the scales in the direction of post-traumatic success and growth. If there is less connection in those areas, post-traumatic stress is more common. Also, if one becomes more compassionate and softened toward oneself and others in the wake of life crises or traumas, one is more likely to benefit from that terrible experience. Finally, if one can take the trauma and use it to find a way to contribute to the world and others, growth is more likely to happen than post-traumatic problems.

Exercise

Think of some trauma or crisis you (the therapist) have had in your life. List the positive and negative things that have come to you as a direct or indirect result of going through that experience.

Then try the same exercise with a client. Explain that bad experiences sometimes have good and bad effects. Ask them to consider what good things as well as troubles have come from going through whatever trauma or crisis that has brought them to therapy. Use that as a jumping-off place for discussions of how they could continue their post-traumatic growth and diminish the post-traumatic stress after-effects.

External Resource

There is a free inventory available to help assess post-traumatic benefits. It is called the Post-Traumatic Growth Inventory (or PTGI). It might be helpful to send your clients to the website where they can take this inventory for no charge and then discuss the results afterward in session.

The website: http://cust-cf.apa.org/ptgi/

References

Affleck, G., Tennen, H., Croog, S., & Levine, S. (1987). Causal attribution, perceived benefits, and morbidity following a heart attack. *Journal of Consulting and Clinical Psychology, 55,* 29–35.

O'Hanlon, B. (2004). *Thriving through crisis: Turning tragedy and trauma into growth and change.* New York: Penguin/Perigee.

To Forgive Is Divine

Overview

"Forgive," according to *Webster's New World Dictionary,* means: "to give up resentment against or the desire to punish; pardon; to overlook an offense." There is research that indicates those who hold resentments, grudges, and anger toward others are less happy. But forgiveness is not easy to do, in part because people confuse some issues around forgiving. Robert Enright, Ph.D., an educational psychologist at the University of Wisconsin-Madison, stresses that true forgiveness is not

- **Forgetting:** If the hurt wounded you enough to require forgiveness, you may always have a memory of it.
- **Excusing or condoning:** The wrong should not be denied, minimized, or justified.
- **Reconciling:** You can forgive the offender and still choose not to reestablish the relationship.
- **Weakness:** You do not become a doormat or oblivious to cruelty.

E. L. Worthington (1997), noted forgiveness researcher, has compiled some of the findings regarding the benefits of forgiveness. The act of forgiveness can result in less anxiety, less depression, better health outcomes, increased coping with stress, and increased feelings of closeness to God and others.

A recent study (Tibbits et al., 2006) of 25 patients with diagnosed stage-1 hypertension who received forgiveness training found that the subjects undergoing forgiveness training achieved significant reductions in anger expression when compared to the control group. Participants who started the program more angry achieved significant reductions in blood pressure.

Another study (Reed & Enright, 2006) involved 20 women who had been emotionally abused in relationships. They were assigned to either forgiveness training or training in anger validation, assertiveness, and interpersonal skill building. Women in the forgiveness group showed significantly greater improvement in trait anxiety, PTSD, self-esteem, amount of forgiveness, environmental mastery, and finding meaning in suffering. Paradoxically, holding a grudge or seeking revenge can backfire on the resentful one. Actress and writer Carrie Fisher has said: "Resentment is like drinking poison and waiting for the other person to die."

Carlsmith, Gilbert, and Wilson (2008) created an experiment with a planted confederate in a group who took financial advantage of the others in the group. After being taken advantage of, participants were given the opportunity to financially punish the offender and were asked before they did so how they thought getting revenge would make them feel. They all predicted it would be cathartic and would make them feel better. But in fact, they ended up feeling worse. They ruminated about the person and the wrong more when they sought revenge. Those who forwent revenge minimized the wrong and moved on.

Suggestions for Use

This exercise is primarily for clients who are angry and resentful toward others—those clients who regularly bring up hurts and slights from someone in their past or current life and haven't forgiven or moved on substantially from an old injury.

Exercise

For this exercise, have the client complete the following steps.

1. Ask the client to come up with a list of several people against whom he (she) holds a grudge and has thought about revenge or bad things happening to that person.
2. Next, have the client write a letter to any or all of those people, not necessarily to send, but just to express and record his (her) resentments and declare his (her) willingness to forgive that person and let the resentment go.

    If the client decides it is appropriate after writing the letter and discussing it with you in session, he (she) could send an edited version to the person he (she) forgave.

Finally, we leave you with a quotation from Josh Billings:

"There is no revenge so complete as forgiveness."

References

Carlsmith, G., Gilbert, D., & Wilson, T. (2008). The paradoxical consequence of revenge. *Journal of Personality and Social Psychology, 95*(6), 1316–1324.

Reed, G. L., & Enright, R. D. (2006). The effects of forgiveness therapy on depression, anxiety, and posttraumatic stress for women after spousal emotional abuse. *Journal of Consulting and Clinical Psychology, 74*, 920–929.

Tibbits, D., Ellis, G., Piramelli, C., Luskin, F., & Lukman, R. (2006). Hypertension reduction through forgiveness training. *Journal of Pastoral Care and Counseling, 60*(1-2), 27–34.

Worthington, E. L. (Ed.). (1997). *Dimensions of forgiveness: Psychological research and theological perspectives.* West Conshohocken, PA: Templeton Foundation Press.

Additional Resources

Finkel, E. J., Burnette, J. L., & Scissors, L. S. (2007). Vengefully ever after: Destiny beliefs, state attachment anxiety, and forgiveness. *Journal of Personality and Social Psychology, 92*, 871–886.

McCullough, M. E., Bono, G., & Root, L. M. (2007). Rumination, emotion, and forgiveness: Three longitudinal studies. *Journal of Personality and Social Psychology, 92*, 490–505.

For more on this subject, visit http://www.loveandforgive.org/ and http://www.forgiving.org/.

Every Generation

Overview

People of every generation face existential questions related to the nature of being, meaning, isolation, freedom, death, and so on. Although the questions people ask of themselves vary according to culture, society, family, etc., no one is exempt from questions about life. For those persons who live in more industrialized areas of the world, the onslaught of up-to-the-minute information is constant. There are 24-hour news stations feeding the latest-breaking stories, interruptions to programs through tickers that parade across the bottom of television screens, and mobile phones that keep us up-to-date when we are in transit. With our senses bombarded with what amounts to mostly negative news, it can be challenging to focus on "what's good about life" and to make sense of what happens in the world. This purpose of this exercise is to explore existential questions that evoke hope, well-being, and optimism about the future.

Suggestions for Use

This exercise is for all persons—both clients and therapists. As a therapist, you may want to try this exercise before recommending for a client (we suggest this with every exercise in this book). Talk with the client about the concept of everyday themes that pass from one generation to the next. Examples include isolation, loneliness, meaning, and death. When talking about life themes, consider those that are not situational and continue throughout life. For example, no one is exempt from death. Every society faces the threat of war, whether internal or external. It is recommended that the focus is on one issue at a time so as to not overwhelm the client; however, this decision should be made on a client-by-client basis.

Exercise

This exercise will help you explore the more positive side of life themes that often evades us when we focus on everyday events, particularly those portrayed in the media. To complete this exercise, follow the steps below.

1. Begin by reviewing the list of themes that affect every generation. In the space next to the themes, write what each one means to you. Once you have finished, consider adding themes that you believe extend from one generation to the next.

Isolation: _____

_____

Freedom: _____

_____

Meaning: _____

_____

Death: _____

_____

Loneliness: _____

_____

_____: _____
         _____

_____: _____
         _____

_____: _____
         _____

_____: _____
         _____

2. Next, review the themes listed in Step 1 and write any resulting emotions in the space below.

_____
_____
_____
_____
_____

3. Take a moment to reflect on your responses in Step 2. What percentage were negative emotions? How about positive emotions? One of our ongoing challenges is to face the existential themes that come with living. While we may or may not be able to influence external factors and situations, we can influence how we think and feel about those things.

   Consider the themes listed under Step 1 as "conditions of life" and representative of those things with which all humans must cope. Next, think about the themes through an unconditional lens of hope, optimism, happiness, joy, connection, and love.
   Next, in the space below, write whatever spontaneous positive emotions, feelings, reactions, or sensations you have.

_____
_____
_____
_____
_____

4. How might the reactions you documented in Step 3 help you in the future, particularly as you face those themes and issues that persist throughout life? Consider that your response to these themes is something you can influence, anytime you want. Talk with your therapist about what you have learned and how you can continue to reap the benefits of positive emotions in the face of life's challenges.

Sailing the Three Cs of Spirituality

Overview

Religion and spirituality play a role in many people's lives to give meaning and purpose by connecting people with something beyond themselves and a moral compass for their conduct. But religion has also been used to justify cruelty and violence, and people often disagree to the death about whose religion is right and whose is wrong (or evil).

To include this important area, but to steer away from partisan bickering, we are including spirituality as the broader term. We define spirituality with three elements we call the three Cs: Connection, Compassion, and Contribution.

Connection: Most religious or spiritual approaches help people connect with something bigger within and beyond themselves. We have identified seven pathways for connection to something bigger within oneself and beyond oneself:

1. Connection to one's soul / spirit / deeper self / core self
2. Connection to one's physical self / body / senses
3. Connection to one other being (human or animal / pet)
4. Connection to a group or community
5. Connection through art (creating or observing / participating in art created by others)
6. Connection to nature (and the sense of being part of something bigger than oneself)
7. Connection to God / one's higher power / the universe and a bigger sense of meaning or purpose

Compassion: Another element is to help people soften, to become less harsh, less angry, and less judgmental toward themselves and others.

Contribution: Being of service to others or the world. Doing something that does not directly benefit you, but is more altruistic.

Suggestions for Use

This exercise is primarily for clients. Because religion or spirituality can be such a source of purpose, can offer solace, and can provide resources to help people cope and make positive changes, a few questions to assess whether any of those aspects are available to help in the therapy process might be warranted. Be careful not to impose your own religious or spiritual beliefs on people and tread gently in this potentially sensitive area, but do not leave it out.

Exercise

Here are some areas to examine and questions to consider asking regarding **Connection**:

- Do you feel connected to something bigger than petty or selfish concerns? Are you working or living for money alone, for status alone, or is there some bigger, less ego-concerned purpose?
- Is there ample opportunity for you in your life to reconnect with something bigger when you are feeling depleted or getting petty? Is there a chance for connecting through one of the seven pathways discussed above?

The second C is **Compassion**. This is the place where we can feel love toward others, and there is a softening of the usual mistrust, harshness, or judgmental attitude we usually feel.

Here are some areas to examine and questions to consider regarding **Compassion**:

- Does your life create an atmosphere of compassion, rather than being judgmental or harsh? How could you create or enhance an atmosphere of compassion and kindness?
- If this person (or you) were your child or best friend, how would you view them or relate to them?
- Think of the most serene, compassionate, or wise person or figure you know. How would he (she) view this situation or deal with it?
- Remember a time when you were judgmental or critical of someone and then softened or were more compassionate. How did you make that shift? What changed after you made that shift? Can you apply any of that to your current situation?

The third C is **Contribution** or Service. Usually this comes out of the first two Cs. When we feel connected to something beyond our petty, self-concerned selves and when we feel connected, we are usually moved to make a contribution to others and to the world and to be of service.

Here are some areas to examine to consider regarding **Contribution**:

- Become aware of some social injustice or victim situation that moves or touches you.
- Every time you experience some recurrent problem, do one thing to contribute to the relief of the victim's suffering or to righting some social injustice. It may be writing a letter, making a donation of money or time to some charitable group, praying, or some other action you are moved to take.

Additional Resource

O'Hanlon, B. (2006). *Pathways to spirituality: Connection, wholeness, and possibility for therapist and client.* New York: W. W. Norton.

Mitzvah Therapy

Overview

Bill first heard the term "Mitzvah Therapy" from the late psychologist Sol Gordon. Dr. Gordon told a story about a client who had been referred to him because she wasn't making any progress in therapy for her sexual abuse issues after spending five years in treatment with one therapist and then another four years with a second therapist. She remained miserable. She was skilled in her work, but it didn't provide much meaning. Outside of work, she compensated for her misery by overeating.

After hearing her story, Dr. Gordon looked her in the eye and said, "I would have referred you to either of those therapists. They do good work with sexual abuse issues. I don't think any more psychotherapy will help you." She was a bit crestfallen. "You mean you don't think there is any help for me?" "No, I didn't say that," Dr. Gordon replied. "I recommend Mitzvah Therapy." He explained that mitzvahs were good deeds done by someone with no expectations of rewards or thanks. He recommended she find a treatment center for abused and neglected kids. They were always understaffed, underfunded, and overwhelmed. On her time off, she should volunteer as often as she could at one of these places, doing anything they needed, whether it was sweeping the floors, filing, answering the phone, or whatever. She agreed to try it and returned in a month, as they had agreed.

> This Mitzvah Therapy is amazing, Dr. Gordon. You were right. This is helping me much more than psychotherapy ever did. I found a treatment center and they did need me. They asked me to come there several nights a week (and I have started going in on Saturdays as well). All they needed me to do was to sit with the children while the overworked staff answered long-overdue calls and got to long-neglected paperwork.
>
> When I arrive at the center, not only am I greeted by the smiling faces of the relieved staff, but the children come to me like moths to the flame. I'm just there to listen to them and give them love. But as much love as I am giving out, I find that I am getting much more back. I have so much love to give and have not had a place to give it before. I feel as if I am worthwhile for the first time in my life.

Suggestions for Use

There is a line in Rick Warren's (2007) book entitled *The Purpose-Driven Life*, which reads, "It's not about you!" Of course, most psychotherapy is all about the client, but sometimes that focus is either not helping or is part of the problem. Using the idea of Mitzvah Therapy, we can encourage clients to focus outside themselves and do something for someone else or the world. Of course, it may be even more powerful to find a link between their act of service and kindness and the way in which they are troubled. The client in Dr. Gordon's case above identified with the wounded children with whom she worked. Helping to care for them went some distance toward healing her own wounds.

Exercise

One way to implement the idea of Mitzvah Therapy is to connect the client's symptoms with moving them into doing some social good in the world. Here's one possibility. Tell your client:

- Become aware of some social injustice or victim situation that moves or touches you.
- Every time you experience your recurrent problem, do one thing to contribute to the relief of the victim's suffering or to righting that social injustice. It may be writing a letter, making a

donation of money or time to some charitable group, praying, or some other action you are moved to take.

• Try this for a few weeks and notice what difference it makes. It may take a little tweaking or changing the focus or type of contribution you are making to notice the best effect.

Reference

Warren, R. (2007). *The purpose-driven life.* Grand Rapids, MI: Zondervan.

Making Amends

Overview

There is a long tradition in Alcoholics Anonymous and other "12-step" self-help groups to make amends for the wrongs one has done or the injuries one has caused. Many participants in these groups have recounted the power of making amends. It may be in the form of an apology; it may involve restitution. Making amends can be a way to find closure, to relieve guilt or shame, and to move out of a personal to an interpersonal or social focus.

Cloé Madanes once talked about working with a man who had been physically abusive to his wife. After the abuse stopped, they discussed the damage that had been done and what he could do to make amends. She suggested he make a donation, for an amount "that hurt," to a battered women's shelter. That way, not only had he apologized and done something to make things up to his wife, but he was contributing to healing societal wounds and this helping to mend the social fabric he was part of rending.

All around the world, truth and reconciliation panels have been set up after major genocides and social violence has subsided in an attempt to heal the social fabric. These involve telling the truth and asking for forgiveness from those one has wronged or harmed (whether it is granted or not is not guaranteed). Again, participants in this process, both those who confess wrong and those who hear those confessions, report a powerful healing effect from the process.

Eugene de Kock, the commanding officer of state-sanctioned apartheid death squads, is currently serving 212 years in jail for crimes against humanity. As part of the truth and reconciliation process, he met with the widows of many of the men he had tortured and killed. He told the women the truth about what had happened to their husbands and asked them for their forgiveness. Because they had never known what happened, they were grateful for the information and closure, and also could tell by his demeanor that he was genuinely regretful for and pained by what he had done. The widows and de Kock ended up crying together, and the women sincerely forgave him. Pumla Gobodo-Madikizela (2004), a South African psychologist who facilitated the meeting and served on the South African Truth and Reconciliation panel, recounts this and other moving stories in her book, *A Human Being Died that Night...*, if you'd like to read more about the process of making apologies and amends.

Suggestions for Use

Making amends is especially powerful when clients have come through a challenging time in which they did things of which they were ashamed, feel guilty about, or acted out in ways that hurt or harmed others. Sometimes this method involves writing letters of apology; sometimes it involves making anonymous donations; sometimes it involves confessing some wrong or making an apology in person. It might involve restitution. The heart of the matter is recognizing and acknowledging something one has done that one feels bad about and making some effort to make things right.

Exercise

To complete this exercise, have the client take the following steps.

1. Have the client make a list of those whom he (she) has wronged or hurt.
2. Have the client examine the list for accountability and honesty, and rewrite it if necessary.
3. Have the client write a practice letter or role-play with you talking with the person or people he (she) has wronged or hurt. Do not have the client do this in real life unless you have discussed it thoroughly and thought of as many possible scenarios as you can about what might happen

in response to such an approach. Sometimes it might cause more pain and damage to proceed with making contact with the wronged party. The purpose is not just to find relief or assuage guilt for the client, but also to create some healing for the wronged person. Balance these goals carefully and err on the side of caution and protecting the victim.

4. It may be that the best way to make amends is anonymously. It might be a silent prayer; it might be a donation; it might be a random act of kindness.

Reference

Gobodo-Madikizela, P. (2004). *A human being died that night: A South African woman confronts the legacy of apartheid.* New York: Mariner Books.

In Their Footsteps

Overview

This exercise is to help clients to draw meaning from those who came before them. These persons could be ancestors, historical figures, or any known or unknown person who provides a source of inspiration. The purpose of this exercise is for clients to connect with the thoughts, feelings, and actions portrayed by persons of interest and to import those experiences into life in the present and future.

Suggestions for Use

This exercise is for all persons—clients and therapists. As a therapist, you may want to try out the exercise before recommending it to a client (we suggest this with every exercise in this volume). Talk with the client about the various sources in life from which he (she) draws inspiration. In this instance, ask the client to focus on persons as opposed to nature, or music, or some other element of life. The idea is to help the client connect with the life of the person(s) identified to draw inspiration and meaning that can be helpful in the present and future.

Exercise

This exercise will help you to identify persons from whom you can draw inspiration and meaning to better face the circumstances of life in the present and future. To complete this exercise, follow the steps below.

1. Take a few moments to think of persons—ancestors, historical figures, known or unknown person—whom you admire or draw inspiration or meaning from. Write (in the left-hand column) the names of the persons who come to mind.

Person   Key Words

_____   _____

_____   _____

_____   _____

_____   _____

_____   _____

_____   _____

_____   _____

_____   _____

_____   _____

2. Next, in the right-hand column of Step 1, jot down any key words that come to mind when you think about each person of note. In particular, consider how these persons inspire you.
3. Think of a current challenge you are facing. Describe the challenge or problem in the space below.

_____

_____

_____

_____

4. Consider how two or more of the persons you listed in Step 1 might view the challenge you described. Write any key words that capture the essence of these persons' perspectives.

Person   View

_____   _____

_____   _____

_____   _____

_____   _____

5. Reflect on the following questions and share your responses with your therapist if that is helpful.
   • How can one or more of the views you listed influence the way you are currently thinking about or approaching the challenge you are experiencing?
   • How can you draw inspiration from these differing perspectives?
   • How might you use what you have learned in the future?
   • How can you use this exercise in the future should you face the same or a different challenge?
   • What might those who have inspired you say about how you approach the future?
   • How might you be an even greater influence on others who face various challenges in life?

Appreciative Inquiry: Finding Meaning and Strengths at Work

Overview

Concurrent with and parallel to the development of solution-based approaches to therapy and Positive Psychology empirically investigating the brighter side of human existence, a similar approach arose in organizational development. Appreciative Inquiry was originally developed by David Cooperrider and colleagues (Cooperrider & Whitney, 2005).

Appreciative Inquiry, unlike many "expert" and problem-oriented approaches to organizational change, focuses on the discovery of solutions that already exist in the organization, what is working in the workplace, and reflecting and amplifying those aspects to move the group in positive directions.

Implementing Appreciative Inquiry involves the 4-D process facilitated by a trained consultant:

- **Discover:** In this phase, the group and consultant seek to discover what is working well in the organization.
- **Dream:** In this phase of the inquiry, participants and the consultant jointly investigate people's individual and group hopes and longings for the organization into the future.
- **Design:** Small groups come up with plans to realize part or all of the dreams, hopes, and longings uncovered in the Dream phase. The small groups check back in with the larger group to tweak and clarify the plans.
- **Delivery:** The plans and actions decided are implemented, checking in regularly to ensure they are on track and adjustments made as necessary.

Suggestions for Use

Because many of our clients spend so much time at work and some of us as therapists are called to consult in problematic workplaces when there are personal conflicts, we thought this section might be helpful for us to examine a Positive Psychology approach to organizations and workplaces. Who knows, you might even use it with your own organization or workplace to shift things into a more positive direction.

Questions to Ask

Ask your client some of the questions that follow to discover what works and what their hopes and dreams about their workplace are. You might also consider writing down the client's responses.

- What was the best moment you have had working there so far? What made it so good?

  _____

  _____

- Can you recall a time when you resolved a workplace problem that had been very challenging? What happened? What did you do that helped create the solution?

  _____

  _____

- Was there a time that you received really good supervision or support from someone at work? Tell me about that.

_____

_____

- What is the most important lesson you have learned working here so far?

_____

_____

- Talk about a time when you felt your voice or view was really heard on the job.

_____

_____

- When have you been the most pleasantly surprised by something that happened at your place of work?

_____

_____

- Who have you admired on this job? What have you admired about them or the way they handle things?

_____

_____

- Tell me about a time when you felt really valued on the job.

_____

_____

- Tell me about a time when you worked out a conflict with someone at work.

_____

_____

- When have you felt most moved by something that happened at work?

_____

_____

- When have you felt most a part of your work organization?

_____

_____

• When do you think your strengths or skills have been best utilized there?

_____

_____

• What kind of workplace or organization do you think your workplace could become if it followed its best path and brought out the best in everyone there?

_____

_____

• What kind of environment would help you thrive?

_____

_____

• If this place really worked, what would be happening?

_____

_____

• What are your dreams for the organization?

_____

_____

• If you were put in charge, what changes would you implement that you think would make this place better and more successful?

_____

_____

Reference

Cooperrider, D. L., & Whitney, D. (2005). *Appreciative inquiry: A positive revolution in change.* San Francisco, CA: Berrett-Koehler Publishers.

Resource

Hammond, S. A. (1998) *The thin book of appreciative inquiry* (2nd ed.). Plano, TX: Thin Book Publishing Company.

Building a Better Place

Overview

Most community-based settings face similar external challenges. These include factors such as threats to funding, employee turnover, and long client wait-lists. But internal threats arguably pose the greatest threats to an organization's vitality. And perhaps the greatest of these is the culture of the organization. The purpose of this exercise is to help organizations reexamine their cultural philosophies and take steps toward increasing well-being among employees. This process helps to build positive institutions and benefit multiple entities by improving services to clients and increasing the well-being of staff.

Suggestions for Use

This exercise can be carried out in small groups of two or more persons or in larger institutions. In larger institutions, it is advisable that as many levels of leadership and service providers as possible be included from the outset. Organizational change requires a commitment from persons at all levels. It is further recommended that a plan be established for disseminating any changes in ways that create opportunities for feedback from those who may not be directly involved. Patience is also an important virtue in reexamining the current climate of an organization and determining what, if anything, should change.

Exercise

For this exercise, assemble a group of persons to represent the organization. Next, follow the steps listed below.

1. As a group, consider the following overarching ideas:
   - Every practice or organization has strengths and something that works.
   - What is focused on and given attention becomes a socially constructed reality.
   - There are many perspectives and ways to understand a situation.
   - Respect toward others and in relationships facilitates cooperation.
   - Every organization needs a collective vision.

   Have the group reflect on these ideas and note any comments in the space below:

   _____

   _____

   _____

   _____

   _____

   _____

   _____

   _____

   _____

   _____

2. Using the questions in this section as a guide, identify current strengths of the practice or organization and write those strengths in the space below:
   • What are the strengths and gifts of the practice or organization?
   • What has contributed to the strengths and gifts of the practice or organization?
   • What gives the practice or organization spirit and life?
   • What does the practice or organization do well as a whole?
   • How can the practice or organization as a whole keep up the good work?
   • How can the practice or organization as a whole develop those good practices even further?

   Practice/Organization's Strengths

   • _____
   • _____
   • _____
   • _____
   • _____
   • _____
   • _____
   • _____
   • _____
   • _____

3. Next, consider the practice or organization's strengths relative to the questions below and document in the space below any reflections that result from the group's conversation.
   • How are staff strengths identified and utilized?
   • How are relationships honored and valued within the practice or organization?
   • How are everyday dilemmas approached from a strengths-based perspective?

   _____
   _____
   _____
   _____
   _____
   _____
   _____
   _____
   _____

4. Take what has been documented in Steps 1 through 3 and discuss it with others within the organization whose voices may not have been represented during this process. In the space below, write any themes that emerge from the feedback of such persons or groups.

_____

_____

_____

_____

_____

_____

_____

_____

_____

_____

5. For this final section, based on the overall themes from this exercise, list five things that the practice or organization will do to *better* deliver its strengths both internally and externally.

    1. _____

    2. _____

    3. _____

    4. _____

    5. _____

6. Continue to reflect on how the practice or organization will continue to examine its underlying philosophical ideologies.

Resources

Bertolino, B. (2010). *Strengths-based engagement and practice: Creating effective helping relationships.* Boston, MA: Allyn & Bacon.

Bertolino, B., Kiener, M. S., & Patterson, R. (2009). *The therapist's notebook for strengths and solution-based therapies: Homework, handouts, and activities.* New York: Routledge/ Taylor & Francis.

Optimism and Orientation

In this chapter we examine and offer exercises for one of the key areas in Positive Psychology. It turns out that optimism can help people stay out of depression, or if they develop it, can help them have a shorter and less severe course of depression. Because depression decreases happiness levels, this orientation toward a more hopeful future is important in applying Positive Psychology with clients.

Indeed, if one thinks about it, much of the progress for human civilization is built on a sense of optimism (even delusional optimism at times). Dr. Martin Luther King famously said, "Everything that is done in the world is done by hope." By this, we don't mean to diminish the importance of pessimism, skepticism, or negativity. They all have their place in one's emotional life and in life in general. We think a proper balance between optimism, hope, future-mindedness, and a firm grounding in the present and the past as well as a hard-minded skepticism is a good stance. But in this chapter we focus on the more optimistic and hopeful side of things.

Learned Optimism

Overview

Martin Seligman, the consolidator of Positive Psychology, studied the optimism-pessimism spectrum before he became a Positive Psychology researcher. Seligman (2006) showed that having a pessimistic explanatory bias was correlated with getting depressed and longer courses of depression, and that those explanatory styles were fairly stable over the course of a life.

Of course, people do fall somewhere on a continuum, but if one was on the pessimistic side of that spectrum, he and other researchers discovered that when difficult things happened in life, more pessimistic people have the sense that bad "stuff" is

- Permanent and will persist
- Pervasive
- Out of their control

More than this, that bad stuff reflects

- Their resourcelessness
- Bad qualities or character ("I'm such a loser.")

In contrast, more optimistic people think that when bad stuff happens, it is

- Time limited ("I am just going through a rough patch.")
- Context limited ("This just is terrible.")
- Under their influence ("I can do something about this.")

Optimistic persons also tend to think of themselves as possessing good and resourceful qualities. And the good news is that, although these explanatory styles tend to remain stable over time, they can be changed by deliberate activities. One study (Seligman, Stern, Park, & Peterson, 2005) found that even naturally pessimistic people who spent one week doing exercises in which they did one of the tasks listed below were happier when their happiness levels were measured six months later:

- Identified and wrote down times in the past in which they were at their best
- Wrote down their personal strengths
- Expressed gratitude to someone they had never properly thanked
- Wrote down three good things that happened that day

Research has shown that people are capable of increasing their levels of optimism and happiness over the course of their lives. The purpose of this exercise is to encourage a flexible and more optimistic mind-set.

Suggestions for Use

This is an exercise for use with clients although therapists can also practice using the ideas to create more of an optimistic perspective.

Now that we know about brain plasticity—the capability of the brain to develop flexible functioning all through life—we know that repeating thoughts or focus of attention or activities can make us better and more efficient at whatever we repeat and practice. It turns out that explanatory styles can be shifted through the practice of challenging one's current explanatory tendencies and substituting the other. Here is a sample dialogue that might happen in a session illustrating this shift.

> *Client:* I'm such a loser. I blew it again. I'll never get a date again.
> *Therapist:* It could be, but I suspect it is more complicated than that. Perhaps this wasn't the right kind of person for you or perhaps you approached her in the wrong way. Let's talk about those things before we decide that you will be alone forever.

Exercise

For this exercise, do the following:

- If you notice that your client tends to use pessimistic explanatory styles when troubles happen or to explain what has gone wrong in the past, gently challenge them when you hear those explanations.

For example, you might say, "I wonder if there are other ways we might think of your situation. What ideas do you have about that?" (As a therapist you might then offer an alternative or two). You could say, "Some people might wonder if _____?" "Other people might explain what's happening as _____?" Take care to not invalidate the person and his (her) experience.

- When your client generalizes or attributes negative and fixed characteristics to himself (herself), acknowledge that as one possibility and then gently probe to get more specific details of the problem situation and use those to introduce the possibility that there is a different (and more optimistic, or more changeable) way to see it.

For example, you might say, "I see where you are coming from. That's one possibility. What I also heard you say about your situation is_____. That leads me to wonder if _____. What do you think about that?"

Remember to never invalidate your clients, tell them that they are wrong, or argue with them. This method, when done smoothly and well, will be barely noticeable to most clients. Accepting their initial report as one way to see things, rather than the wrong way to see things, is the key to using this method skillfully.

References

Seligman, M. (2006). *Learned optimism: How to change your mind and your life.* New York, NY: Vintage.

Seligman, M., Stern, T., Park, N., & Peterson, C. (2005). Positive psychology progress: Empirical validation of interventions. *American Psychologist, 60,* 410–421.

Personal Benchmarking

Overview

In business, there is a practice called "benchmarking." It involves studying best practices from one's own company, from competitors' companies, or from people in different fields. By having a clear idea of benchmarks and knowing how those benchmarks compare with others, companies can identify what works, what does not, and work to improve from their baselines. The concept of benchmarking can also be useful to clients. This exercise is to help clients in two ways. The first is to identify what clients do well in any certain area, or how they cope best with problems. The second is to make a list of attitudes, points of view, where clients focus their attention, what actions they take, who they interact with, how they think, where they spend time, and other things that are happening during these best practice moments.

Suggestions for Use

This exercise is applicable to all clients but can be particularly useful for those who have a bit of a "competitive side." To set up this exercise, it may be helpful to talk with clients about the concept of personal benchmarks. One way to do this is to introduce the idea that by knowing one's own baseline, it is easier to identify improvement. For example, if a golfer doesn't ever keep score, he (she) will not know how well he (she) is doing. A good place to start is by identifying what one does well. From there, steps can be identified for improvement.

Exercise

For the first part of this exercise, think of the best moments of your life, or the times when you have dealt with difficulties in a way that worked or of which you felt proud. When thinking of those times, capture some skills and aspects from those times to use in everyday life or when you are faced with a problem by writing your responses in the space provided below.

In those better moments or times:

• How were you thinking or how do you think?

_____

_____

_____

_____

_____

• On what did/do you focus your attention?

_____

_____

_____

_____

_____

• What did/do you do differently than when things weren't/aren't going so well?

_____

_____

_____

_____

_____

• Who do you tend to be around and spend time with (or are you usually alone)?

_____

_____

_____

_____

_____

• Where do you spend time?

_____

_____

_____

_____

_____

• Anything else that is different you might be able to use from those moments?

_____

_____

_____

_____

_____

• Looking back over your answers, what do you notice about what you do well?

_____

_____

_____

_____

_____

• What could you do to with this information to improve just a little bit from your past successes?

_____

_____

_____

_____

_____

• How can you continue to grow, improve, and build on your baseline success?

_____

_____

_____

_____

_____

Your Best Possible Self

Overview

Subjects in an experiment (Sheldon & Lyubomirsky, 2006) were instructed to spend time visualizing and writing about their best possible future selves. Here's what they were told:

You have been randomly assigned to think about your best possible self now, and during the next few weeks. "Think about your best possible self" means that you imagine yourself in the future, after everything has gone as well as it possibly could. You have worked hard and succeeded at accomplishing all of your life goals. Think of this as the realization of your life dreams, and of your own best potentials. In all of these cases, you are identifying the best possible way that things might turn out in your life, in order to help guide your decisions now. You may not have thought about yourself in this way before, but research suggests that doing so can have a strong positive effect on your mood and life satisfaction. So, we'd like to ask you to continue thinking in this way over the next few weeks, following up on the initial writing that you're about to do."

After four weeks, they were found to have more positive emotions than control subjects. The purpose of this exercise is to help increase positive emotion with clients through visualization.

Suggestions for Use

This method is designed to orient people to their positive future rather than the past or problems. It seems as if this orientation, like many perspectives, can be ingrained more deeply with practice and deliberate effort. Modern brain science, with its discovery of brain plasticity, shows us that repeating thoughts or focus of attention or activities can make us better and more efficient at whatever we repeat and practice.

Using this method and having the client repeat it for some time can help orient (or reorient) clients to a more positive future.

Exercise

For this exercise, first have clients discuss their sense or vision of their best possible future self—a future in which things went well. Document that vision in the space provided.

Next, ask the following questions, again writing the client's responses in the space provided.

• What would that future self be doing?

- How would that future self be feeling?

_____

_____

_____

- How would that future self be relating to others?

_____

_____

_____

Suggest that your client try an experiment for several weeks after the session in which this issue is discussed. If possible, they should write about this "best possible future self" for some time each night and spend time thinking about themselves in this way when they have a spare moment so that the details are filled out as fully as possible.

After the several weeks pass, have another discussion with your client about what they got out of the exercise.

Reference

Sheldon, K., & Lyubomirsky, S. (2006). How to increase and sustain positive emotion: The effects of expressing gratitude and visualizing best possible selves. *The Journal of Positive Psychology*, *1*(2), 73–82.

As If

Overview

It takes courage to employ a new or modified strategy in life. Sometimes it is made easier by having the client create a vision of what he (she) would like to have different and then act "as if" that vision has happened. The purpose of this exercise is to ask clients to experiment or "pretend" that their lives are improved in some way, however small, and to experience their lives anew in the face of these positive changes. It is hoped that through this process the client will experience more positive emotion, meaningful existence, connection to others, or accomplishment.

Suggestions for Use

This exercise can be helpful to all clients, but particularly those who express apprehension about trying a new strategy or taking action to make deliberate changes to their lives. This exercise is to encourage forward movement through what can be deemed an "experiment." To introduce this exercise, ask the client to tap into his (her) imagination to envision a future in which things are better or represent a minimal improvement above their current state. Encourage the client to be creative and develop that vision and then follow up by acting "as if" that future has happened.

Exercise

To complete this exercise, have the client complete the steps that follow.

1. Take whatever time you need to imagine the future you would like to have. In doing so, consider one or more of these questions:
   - What specifically would I like to be happening in my life _____ (e.g., three weeks, six months, one year from now)?
   - What will I be doing in the future that is different than right now?
   - What might I be feeling in that future that is different than the way I feel in the present?
   - How might these changes I have made and the way I feel in the future benefit me? Others?
2. Write a brief description of the future that has been described.

   _____

   _____

   _____

3. Next, talk with the client about "experimenting" or "tinkering" with the vision he (she) has created. Take care to not push the client to move at a pace that is inconsistent with his (her) level of motivation. Instead, for the next week (or until the next session/meeting), encourage the client to "pretend" and act "as if" the part of the vision detailed under Step 2 has already occurred.
4. In the subsequent session, ask the client to report on his (her) experience with acting "as if." Consider asking one or more of the following questions in the follow-up session.
   - What has been the most profound aspect of acting "as if" for the past week?
   - What difference did it make for you?
   - What did you feel or experience that was different or new?
   - When you reflect on the past week, what single positive emotion stands out above the rest?
   - How can you get that to continue after you leave here today?
5. Encourage the client to graduate from acting "as if" to fully integrating his (her) new view.

Positive Expectancy Talk

Overview

The late hypnotherapist/psychiatrist Milton H. Erickson once hypnotized a demonstration subject in a workshop using nothing but expectancy. He announced to the group that he wanted to demonstrate hypnosis and asked for a volunteer. When one came on stage, Erickson asked him to take a seat. Then Erickson just leaned back and looked at the volunteer. After a short time, he (the volunteer) went into trance. Then Erickson began to speak to him about various things he could experience during the trance.

After the demonstration was over, the audience members asked if Dr. Erickson had done "psychic hypnosis," as they didn't see him do anything or hear him speak, yet the volunteer went into trance. Erickson assured them there was nothing psychic involved. He had defined the situation as a demonstration of hypnosis. When the volunteer sat down, everyone fully expected him to go into trance. When Erickson did nothing, the expectation was enough to induce the trance.

In a similar way, but using language, one can invite clients who are more oriented to the past and problems to become more oriented to a positive future. This is done using simple phrases that imply and expect positive changes to occur in the future. For example, one might say to a client who was overdrinking, "After you cut back on your alcohol use, I'll be curious about what changes you will experience in your health or relationships." Or to a client who is cutting herself, "So you haven't found a way to stop cutting yet."

These positive phrases include

- When; will
- How quickly?
- Yet
- So far
- After
- Before

Now, of course, the therapist must be conscious of only assuming things that are positive and they and clients would want to occur. That means one would not want to use these phrases to say things like, "After your next relapse," or "Before you two get into another argument."

This method owes a lot to both Carl Rogers (for the acknowledgment and reflection of people's experience and feelings) and Milton Erickson (for the indirect shifting of attention and frame of reference). This method helps people reorient their attention from what they cannot change (the past) and what hasn't been working (the complaint) to what they can change (the future) and what they would prefer to have happen (their goal or direction or desire). The purpose of this exercise is to help clients shift their attention through these subtle changes in language. If done respectfully and skillfully, most people do not even notice the shift consciously, but many report feeling more hopeful after it is used throughout the interview.

Suggestions for Use

This exercise is a sort of Carl Rogers' active listening method *with a twist*—the twist being a shift to a future focus and hopes and longings rather than problems. When the therapist reflects the client's concern, that reflection has a direction—the future and what we would like to occur and go well. Use this method when clients seem stuck on talking about the past or problems and don't talk much about the positive future.

Of course, if you use this method and get a negative response from the client ("You don't get it; that's never going to happen!"), gently move on and don't push it. There are many other methods and exercises in this book that might work better.

Exercise

For this exercise, consider the following points as you use Positive Expectancy Talk.

- In the next few sessions, make a deliberate effort to use Positive Expectancy Talk.
- Realize that this will probably be a bit awkward at first and won't feel natural; that's okay. Just persist and it should become more smooth and natural.
- Notice what responses your client gives to these reflections. Do they become more future oriented in their perspective or speaking? Do they start talking about change?
- If you and the client like the results you are getting, keep using this with them until it becomes second nature.

Additional Resources

O'Hanlon, B. (2003). *A guide to inclusive therapy.* New York: W.W. Norton.
O'Hanlon, B. (2010). *Quick steps to resolving trauma.* New York: W. W. Norton.

Mind-Set

Overview

The benefits of an optimistic mind-set are widely known. For example, people who see problems as temporary, as part of life and living, and as challenges versus insurmountable barriers, tend to experience fewer emotional lows, more happiness, increased life satisfaction, and greater levels of energy. A further benefit of a positive mind-set is creativity. That is, the adoption of a more optimistic view of self, others, situations, and life events can help one be a more thoughtful and creative when faced with stressors, adversity, or problems. The purpose of this exercise is to help cultivate an optimistic mind-set to serve as a personal resource.

Suggestions for Use

Begin by talking with the client about the benefits of an optimistic mind-set in terms of facing, coping with, and better managing life stressors and challenges. Next, introduce the exercise as an opportunity to develop new ideas and inspire creativity. It is important to let the client know that this exercise is not about moving from a negative to a positive frame of mind. Such a focus can prove invalidating. It can be helpful, although not necessary, to encourage the client to ease into a new and expanded way of viewing the world by first engaging in a "brainstorming" experience. Following this, a specific problem or issue may be identified for which this exercise may prove useful. When discussing this exercise with clients, be sure to go through each step in detail. Finally, this is not an "all-or-nothing" exercise. Even a minor shift in mind-set can result in major changes for a person. Encourage clients to continue to practice developing a new mind-set and to stay with the process.

Exercise

This exercise involves the following steps:

1. Have the client rate his or her sense of optimism on a scale of 1 to 10, in which "1" represents a very minimum level or no optimism and "10" represents extreme optimism. Write the client's rating:
   Beginning Client Optimism Level: _____
2. Have the client take several deep breaths. The client may also choose to close his (her) eyes. Ask the client to focus on something that evokes a sense of calmness or relaxation. Stay with this process for up to five minutes or until the client reports an increase in calmness. Keep in mind that such a state is relative. Clients will vary in their ability to relax.
3. Following this, suggest that the client slowly begin to shift his (her) attention to a recent experience of happiness and optimism. Specifically, ask the client to describe a situation in which he (she) felt a sense of joy and more hopeful about the world. Suggest that the client savor the experience.
4. Next, ask the client to ponder one of the brief scenarios described below. The task is to brainstorm as many ideas as possible to further cultivate an optimistic mind-set. Let the client know that there is more than one solution for a particular scenario.
   a. Brief Scenario 1: In three minutes, think of as many ways as possible that a person might use an ink pen.
   b. Brief Scenario 2: Name three ways that a person might attempt to find new meaning with something that has become routine (e.g., relationships, career, etc.).
   c. Brief Scenario 3: Describe three ways that a person might more fully appreciate the element of water (or earth or sun).

(*Note:* The therapist should write the ideas of the client. If this exercise is being completed by the client alone, have him (her) write the ideas.)

Ideas _____   _____
      _____   _____
      _____   _____
      _____   _____
      _____   _____
      _____   _____
      _____   _____

5. Read back to the client the answers he (she) provided in Step 4. Ask the client to describe any positive emotions experienced. Write the client's responses.

Positive Emotions _____   _____
                  _____   _____
                  _____   _____
                  _____   _____
                  _____   _____

6. Have the client rerate his (her) sense of optimism on a scale of 1 to 10, in which "1" represents a very minimum level or no optimism and "10" represents extreme optimism. Write the client's rating:
   Rerated Client Optimism Level: _____

7. Encourage the client to continue to routinely engage in experiences that create a shift in mind-set and to put the best of those new ideas in motion through action.

8. (If applicable) Have the client use his (her) new mind-set with a specific concern or problem.

Working Backward from the Future in Psychotherapy

Overview

The late psychiatrist/hypnotherapist Milton Erickson had a method he would occasionally use when he was stuck in psychotherapy. He would hypnotize his patient and suggest that therapy had ended a year previously and that the patient was now back for a follow-up visit. Erickson then asked them to tell him what they had done in therapy that was so helpful for them and made the crucial difference. Most patients would give him really good ideas. While they were still in trance, Erickson would suggest they develop amnesia for what they had told him. Erickson would then bring them out of hypnosis and proceed to do the helpful therapeutic interventions the patient had told him about.

Most of us are not so skilled with hypnosis, but we can use a nonhypnotic variation of this method. We can do this by asking clients about what they will be doing when therapy is over and they no longer have the problem(s) that brought them to therapy. The purpose of this exercise is to help clients articulate a vision of "better" in their lives and to help them work toward making that vision a reality.

Suggestions for Use

This exercise is for therapists to use with clients. Most therapy starts and focuses on the past and what gave rise to the problems the client brought in. This exercise orients instead to a hopeful future when the client is free of the problem(s).

Exercise

For this exercise, ask the client the questions listed below to work backward from the future. Space is provided to document the client's responses if that is preferred.

- When we are done with therapy and things are better, what will be happening in your life?

  _____

  _____

  _____

  _____

- What could you do, think, or focus on during the next while that would help you move a little bit in that direction or would at least be compatible with it?

  _____

  _____

  _____

- If your problem disappeared, what would be different?
  - In your relationships?
  - In your daily life?
  - In your thinking or focus of attention?
  - In your actions?

- In any other areas?

  _____

  _____

  _____

  _____

- What part of what you described could you start to implement in the near future?

  _____

  _____

  _____

  _____

Problems into Preferences

Overview

Another method to invite clients to develop future-mindedness and hope is to subtly guide them with simple reflections to orient more to the future and what they long for than the past and what they want to get rid of or solve. This can be done using a method called "Problems into Preferences." This method owes a lot to both Carl Rogers (for the acknowledgment and reflection of people's experience and feelings) and Milton Erickson (for the indirect shifting of attention and frame of reference). The purpose of this exercise is to help people reorient their attention from what they cannot change (the past) and what hasn't been working (the complaint) to what they can change (the future) and what they would prefer to have happen (their goal or direction or desire). If done respectfully and skillfully, most people do not even notice the shift consciously, but many report feeling more hopeful after it is used throughout the interview.

Suggestions for Use

This method has four components. We sometimes think of it as Carl Rogers' active listening method with a twist—the twist being a shift to a future focus and hopes and longings rather than problems. When the therapist reflects the client's concern, that reflection has a direction—the future and what the client wants.

Here are the four components, followed by a brief example of each component.

1. Rephrase from what is unwanted to what is desired or preferred.

Client: I think I'm just too shy to find a relationship. I'm afraid of women and of being rejected.
Therapist: So you'd like to be more comfortable around women and be able to get into a relationship.

2. Redirect from the past or present to the future.

Client: We argue all the time.
Therapist: So you'd like to be able to work out conflicts without having so many arguments and even to have fewer conflicts if possible.

3. Mention the presence of something rather than the absence of something.

Client: He never does anything we ask him to.
Therapist: You'd like to see some cooperation from him.

4. Suggest small increments rather than big leaps.

Client: I can't stand this depression.
Therapist: You'd really like to find some way to feel a bit better and be a bit less depressed.

Exercise

To use this approach, follow the general guidelines as you use the Problems into Preferences approach.

- In the next few sessions, make a deliberate effort to use the Problems into Preferences method.
- Realize that this will probably be a bit awkward at first and won't feel natural; that's okay. Just persist and it should become more smooth and natural.
- Notice what responses your client gives to these reflections. Do they become more future oriented in their perspective or speaking?
- If you and the client like the results you are getting, keep using this until it becomes second nature.

Additional References

Bertolino, B. (2010). *Strengths-based engagement and practice: Creating effective helping relationships.* Boston, MA: Allyn & Bacon.

O'Hanlon, B. (2003). *A guide to inclusive therapy.* New York: W.W. Norton.

O'Hanlon, B. (2010). *Quick steps to resolving trauma.* New York: W. W. Norton.

The Pleasant Life in Triplicate

Overview

The Pleasant Life in Positive Psychology refers to contentment with the past, happiness in the present, and hope for the future. The purpose of this exercise is to help clients connect with all three aspects of time. It is hoped that through this exercise clients can ultimately reflect on the past, experience the present, and envision the future in more positive ways.

Suggestions for Use

This exercise is appropriate for all clients. It is a brief activity that can be done in sessions or by clients outside the office. To introduce the exercise, talk with clients about how they have the ability to alter and change their perceptions based on what they choose to place their attention.

Exercise

To complete this exercise, have the client complete the following steps.

1. Think of a situation, event, or time in the past in which you felt at your best. You can choose a situation, event, or time from the recent past or from a long time ago. Take a moment to remember the experience as best as you can. In the space below, write a brief synopsis of the situation, time, or event. Be sure to include what you felt best about and any positive emotions you experienced.

   _____

   _____

   _____

   _____

   _____

   _____

2. Think of something that is currently happening in your life that you feel very good about. Choose something that is still happening. Take a moment to immerse yourself in the experience. In the space below, write a brief synopsis of what is happening. Be sure to include the positive emotions you also experience.

   _____

   _____

   _____

   _____

   _____

   _____

3. Think of the future. Envision a time a few days, months, or years from now. Take a moment to develop that vision and fill in the details. Immerse yourself in the vision as best as you can.

In the space below, write a brief synopsis of your future vision. Be sure to include what makes you most hopeful or optimistic about your future vision.

_____

_____

_____

_____

_____

_____

4. After you have completed the exercise, take a moment to reflect on what the experience was like for you. You may also want to consider one or more of the following questions:
   - What stood out most for you from this exercise?
   - What did you learn about yourself?
   - What might you do with what you have learned?
   - How can you use this exercise in the future?

The Writing Ritual: Exorcising the Ghosts of the Past through Writing

Overview

There have been many studies and even several books about a process called The Writing Ritual. Clinical trials indicate that writing about painful experiences, even for very short courses of writing, can enhance immune response, reduce recovery times from illness and surgery, and promote physical, psychological, and social well-being.

The main researcher in this area is Jamie Pennebaker (1997). He and his graduate students have conducted studies with grade-school students, people in nursing homes, arthritis patients, medical students, rape victims, new mothers, and prisoners and found similar positive results using this method. Their studies have shown that writing thoughts and feelings about trauma or crises for as little as 15 minutes a day for as few as four or five days has been shown to be correlated with

- Far fewer visits to the student health center for college students
- An increase in T-cells (immune system functioning)
- Increasing the likelihood and rapidity of getting a new job after being laid off
- Reduced anxiety and depression
- Improved grades
- Improved mental and physical health of grade-school students, people in nursing homes, arthritis patients, medical students, rape victims, new mothers, and prisoners after troubling experiences

The purpose of this exercise is to help people leave troubling events in the past so they can be more hopeful and open to new possibilities in the present and the future.

Suggestions for Use

This method can be helpful for people who either haven't expressed their feelings about some traumatic or troubling experience or those who are having trouble doing so. Telling their story, plus expressing their felt sense and reaction to what happened, can be healing, but there is a particular structure that has been found especially healing. This involves a time limit for such expression and some ground rules for writing.

Exercise

Here are the instructions to give to clients about doing the writing ritual.

How to do the writing ritual:

1. Write honestly and openly about your deepest feelings and thoughts about the situation you are in or went through. Make sure you keep these writings private or you may find yourself unconsciously censoring what you write and diluting the effects of the writing. Consider destroying what you wrote after it is complete, again for the same reason. Perhaps make a ritual of the burning or destroying of the writing.
2. Write for a relatively short time, say 15 minutes. This writing is often draining or emotionally difficult. Limiting the time makes it both a bit more tolerable and more likely that you will do it.
3. Write for only four or five days. This time limit seemed to work very well in the experiments that were done. They are not carved in granite, however, and if you find you need more time,

you can take it. One of the points of this limit of a few days is again to contain the experience so it doesn't take over your life.

4. Try to find both a private and unique place to write, somewhere you can be both uninterrupted and someplace that won't be associated with other things or that have the usual smells, sights, and sounds of places you already know well.

5. Don't worry about grammar or spelling or getting it right. Just write.

6. During the writing days, try to use the same time each day or evening to write. It's not crucial, but it can sometimes give your unconscious mind some structure and preparation time if it knows exactly when the writing will take place. This can also help contain the emotions and intrusive thinking that may occur and interfere with your day or evening.

7. Writing seems to be the most powerful; but if for some reason that won't work for you, you could try "writing" by speaking into a tape recorder or a video camera.

8. Ignore these guidelines if you discover something else works better for you. Everyone is unique.

Reference

Pennebaker, J. (1997). *Opening up: The healing power of expressing emotions.* New York: Guilford.

Additional Resources

Lepore, S., & Smyth, J. (2002). *The writing cure: How expressive writing promotes health and emotional well-being.* Washington, DC: American Psychological Association.

Pennebaker, J. (2004). *Writing to heal: A guided journal for recovering from trauma & emotional upheaval.* Oakland, CA: New Harbinger.

Smyth, J., Hockemeyer, J., & Tulloch, H. (2008). Expressive writing and post-traumatic stress disorder: Effects on trauma symptoms, mood states, and cortisol reactivity. *British Journal of Health Psychology, 13,* 85–93.

Smyth, J., Stone, A., Hurewitz, A., & Kaell, A. (1999). Writing about stressful events produces symptom reduction in asthmatics and rheumatoid arthritics: A randomized trial. *Journal of the American Medical Association, 281,* 1304–1309.

A Letter from Your Best Day to Your Bad Days

Overview

When people are feeling depressed, tired, unmotivated, and uninspired, it can be difficult for them to see any ray of light in their sea of despondence. The present day seems a repeat of the one before it and the next day holds little hope of being any different. And yet even in the most difficult of times, there are moments, situations, and sometimes entire days that go *differently*. These exceptions can be pivotal in changing the course of problems and oftentimes lead to long-term solutions. The purpose of this exercise is to help clients capture those moments of exception—when things are *better*—by writing a letter to themselves. These letters can trigger change in the present and serve as ongoing reminders of resiliency.

Suggestions for Use

For some clients, this exercise will be a good fit right away. However, not everyone enjoys writing and it's possible to encounter people who have never written a letter. To introduce this exercise, first ask the client his (her) thoughts about writing. If the participant is shy about writing, unsure of his (her) ability, or appears disinterested, gently encourage an "experiment." It can be helpful to say, "Some people have found it helpful to jot down their thoughts and feelings when they experience a slight lift in mood or when things are going just a little better. They want to capture the moment. This activity is one way to do that. If you give it a try, you might learn something about yourself and find that you have more to say than you originally thought." It can also be helpful to use a brief illustration (of your own or from another person) such as the following:

> One time, in the midst of a bad spell of depression, I had an unexpectedly good day. I felt happy, optimistic, and good. I decided to write myself a letter from that day (and that mood) to my darker days, which I was sure were going to return.

After discussing the activity with the client, proceed to the exercise. Please keep in mind that the activity may need to be modified to suit the client.

Exercise

Write a letter to yourself whenever you feel particularly good, powerful, healthy, or functional. Address yourself in your worst moments and speak to the areas that follow. Your letter need not be lengthy unless you prefer it that way. You can use a separate piece of paper, or there is space provided below if you would like to write your letter on these pages.

- What advice would you give yourself for coping with your worst moments from those better moments?
- What should you keep in mind in your worst moments that you are likely to forget?
- What kinds of activities might help you in your worst moments?
- What could give you hope during this bad time?

Letter to My Future Self

Date _____

Dear _____:

_____
_____
_____
_____
_____
_____
_____
_____
_____
_____
_____
_____
_____
_____
_____
_____
_____
_____
_____
_____
_____
_____
_____
_____
_____
_____
_____
_____
_____
_____
_____
_____
_____

_____

Signature

Letter from the Future

Overview

Many clients who come to therapy have a "future-deficit." That is, they are so riveted by the problematic past or present that their sense of a future with possibilities has collapsed or gone missing. Asking clients about a better future usually yields blank stares from this kind of client.

Participants in a study (King, 2001) were asked to write about their ideal future, in which all had gone well and they had met their desired hopes and goals, for a few minutes on four consecutive days. Control groups were asked to write about a traumatic event that had happened to them for those minutes on four days; another group was asked to write about life goals as well as a trauma; another control group was asked to write about their plans for the day on those four days. Results: The "future-oriented" group reported more subjective well-being after the experiment than the controls; both the trauma and "future-oriented" groups had less illness when followed up five months later.

The purpose of this exercise is to begin to create some future-mindedness with these clients. To do this, we suggest they write a letter to their present selves from a future self who has made it through the difficulties and is in a better place.

Suggestions for Use

You can imagine this method if you think about your present self writing a letter back to some past version of yourself, say from five years ago. What have you learned and gained perspective on in the interim? What things were you worried or frightened about in those days that seem trivial or far away for you today? What problems seemed overwhelming or insurmountable in those days that you did eventually resolve or overcome?

What sage advice would your present self give to that past self?

What comfort or reassurance would your present self give to your past self?

Who were you troubled by, frightened by, or concerned with that now doesn't matter as much?

In a similar way, this method asks your clients to use their imagination to move into a better future and send a letter like that back to their present selves.

Exercise

For this exercise, have clients complete the following steps.

1. Have clients write a letter from their future self to their current self from a place where they are happier and have resolved the issues that are concerning them now.
2. Then say: Describe your life (5 years/2 months/10 years/1 year) from now let your intuition and their response guide the time frame; adjust as necessary.
3. Have clients describe where they are, what they are doing, what they have gone through to get there, and so on.
4. Have clients write about the crucial things they realized or did to get there, or write about some crucial turning points that led to this future.
5. Have clients give themselves some sage and compassionate advice from the future.

Consider using the following questions to guide clients' letter writing:

- What have you learned and gained perspective on since back in [fill in the present date/year]?
- What things were you worried or frightened about in those days that seem trivial or far away for you today?

- What problems seemed overwhelming or insurmountable in those days that you did eventually resolve or overcome?
- What sage advice would your future self give to that present self?
- What comfort or reassurance would your future self give to your present self?
- Who were you troubled by, frightened by, or concerned with that now do not matter as much?

Reference

King, L. A. (2001). The health benefits of writing about life goals. *Personality and Social Psychology Bulletin, 27,* 798–807.

Additional Resource

O'Hanlon, B. (2010). *Quick steps to resolving trauma.* New York: W. W. Norton.

In the Moment

Overview

One of the ways we experience positive emotion is through everyday media that evoke happiness, joy, hope, optimism, and so on. Music is a specific medium that can help boost levels of well-being. In fact, music has been referred to as the soundtrack of our lives. The purpose of this exercise is to help clients become immersed in music in a way that helps them experience a greater sense of connection to themselves. This exercise is about helping clients be more "in the moment" and increase their overall sense of well-being.

Suggestions for Use

This exercise can be helpful to all clients but may not be a good fit for those who are not interested in music. For those whom this exercise is applicable, the therapist should spend time getting to know what kinds of music they enjoy. A person who enjoys music may be partial to certain kinds of music. Encourage the client to try this exercise two or more times a day to develop a habit of immersing himself (herself) in music and experiencing the joy it can bring.

Exercise

To complete this exercise, have the client complete the following steps.

1. Think about the songs or pieces of music that have brought out positive emotions in you. Make a list of those songs in the space below.

_____

_____

_____

_____

_____

_____

_____

_____

2. Next to each song, write a few of the positive emotions that the song typically evokes for you (e.g., happiness, joy, inspiration, optimism, etc.).
3. Make sure you have access to the songs you identified and have a means of playing them at home, in your car, on a walk, etc.
4. Make a plan to listen to two songs consecutively at least two times throughout your day. Be sure to plan these moments at times that you are not going to be interrupted.
5. Listen to the songs you have selected. As you do, let yourself become immersed in the music. Let it fill your body, mind, and soul. Try not to think deliberately about anything in particular, just letting yourself become absorbed in the moment.

6. After listening to two songs, take a couple of minutes to reflect on the positive emotions you felt. Think about how you can carry that emotion with you for a portion of your day. You might even consider humming a few bars from time to time as a reminder.

7. As you think of new songs, add them to your list. You might also find more than two times a day to listen to those songs that raise your level of happiness. And when you feel down, overwhelmed, disconnected in some way, or just not yourself, you can turn on your music and change your emotions.

Freeze Frame

Overview

One of the ways we experience positive emotion is through everyday media that evoke happiness, joy, hope, optimism, and so on. Written words, music, and movies all provide opportunities to become immersed in positive emotion, which in turn can boost levels of well-being. In another exercise in this volume, "In the Moment," we offered a way of using music to enhance well-being. The purpose of this exercise is to connect clients with the written word or cinema.

Suggestions for Use

This exercise can be helpful to all clients. However, not everyone enjoys reading or watching movies. In such cases, it may be better to try a different type of activity from this volume. Talk with the client about the benefits of becoming immersed in positive emotion in terms of increasing well-being, fending off illness, having greater life satisfaction, and so on. Also, talk with the client about his (her) preference for written words (i.e., novels, nonfiction, poetry, lyrics, etc.) or movies. Then proceed with the exercise.

Exercise

To complete this exercise, have the client complete the following steps.

1. Choose a book or movie that you have already seen and really enjoyed. You can also choose a specific passage from a book, a poem, lyrics from a song, or a television show. Write your choice in the space below.

   _____

   _____

2. Next, find a time to read the book or watch the movie. Try to arrange for a time during which you will not be interrupted. Then begin reading the book or watching the movie.
3. When you arrive at a passage or scene in the movie in which you experience positive emotion, proceed through it until the passage ends or the scene changes. Then close the book or turn off the movie.

   Now, sit for a moment and let the emotion grow inside you. Feel it throughout your body. Let the positive emotion take over. "Freeze" the emotion in your experience and stay with it.

   In the space below, write the positive emotions you have experienced.

   _____

   _____

   _____

   _____

   _____

4. When you are ready, read on or continue with the movie until another experience of positive emotion arises for you. Repeat Step 3.

5. At another time, read a lengthy section of the book or watch the movie in its entirety without stopping. Then reflect on your experience and note any differences you feel between stopping periodically and immersing yourself in the moment or continuing on.

Social Connections and Networking

Relationships and social connections are essential to our well-being and happiness. Sociologist Robert Putnam (2000) has documented both the importance and the diminishment of social connections in modern American society. He writes:

> Countless studies document the link between society and psyche: people who have close friends and confidants, friendly neighbors, and supportive co-workers are less likely to experience sadness, loneliness, low self-esteem, and problems with eating and sleeping. The single most common finding from a half century's research on the correlates of life satisfaction, not only in the United States but around the world, is that happiness is best predicted by the breadth and depth of one's social connections. (p. 332)

According to Putnam,

- Shared family dinners and family vacations are down over a third in the past 25 years.
- Having friends over to the house is down by 45% over the past 25 years.
- Participation in clubs and civic organizations is down by over 50% in the past 25 years.
- Church attendance is down by about a third since the 1960s.

Other sociological surveys (McPherson, Smith-Lovin, & Brashears, 2006) concur.

- The average number of people we consider close confidants dropped nearly one-third, from 2.94 in 1985 to 2.09 in 2004.
- The average American has only two close friends.
- One in four Americans (25%) reports that they have no one to confide in.
- Average household size has decreased by about 10% during the past 20 years, to 2.5 people.
- In 1990, more than one in five households were headed by a single parent; in 2006, it was one in three.
- 27 million people in the United States live alone, and that was expected to increase to 29 million by 2010.

The aforementioned trends reflect an unfortunate trend. In this chapter we offer exercises and activities designed to enhance clients' positive social relationships, and thus their well-being and satisfaction. As Positive Psychology researcher Sonja Lyubomirsky (2008) writes: "By far the greatest predictor of happiness in the literature is intimate relationships."

References

Lyubomirsky, S. (2008). *The how of happiness: A scientific approach to getting the life you want.* New York: Penguin.

McPherson, M., Smith-Lovin, L., & Brashears, M. (2006). Social isolation in America: Changes in core discussion networks over two decades. *American Sociological Review, 71,* 353–375.

Putnam, R. (2000). *Bowling alone: The collapse and revival of American community.* New York: Simon & Schuster.

Positives to Negatives Ratio

Overview

Couples researcher John Gottman has been studying couples in his "Love Lab" for 30-plus years and has discovered some patterns about what works with couples to keep them together and getting along well (as well as the opposite). His studies give him a high degree of confidence that he can watch and listen to the couple interacting and predict whether or not they will be together and happy in the future. One of the striking findings from his work has been very consistent and replicated many times. Happily married couples say five positive remarks for every negative remark, even when having conflicts. Couples who are headed for divorce use less than one (0.8) positive remark for every negative one (Gottman, Gottman, & DeClaire, 2006).

Another set of researchers found something similar in their studies of correlates of infidelity after marriage. Couples with a 2.4-to-1 ratio of positive interactions (nodding, smiling, eye contact) to negative interactions (eye-rolling, scowling, expressing contempt) were more likely to experience infidelity after being married than couples with a 4-to-1 positive-to-negative interaction ratio (Allen et al., 2008). This robust finding can be readily translated into clinical work with couples. The purpose of this exercise is to increase the positive-to-negative ratios couples have with each other.

Suggestions for Use

This is one time when we suggest just telling couples (or parents) about this research and suggesting they start implementing it in their intimate relationships. Most people understand this instantly when they are given the research results. Of course, putting it into practice is easier said than done, especially when conflict is high.

Exercise

For this exercise, have couples complete the following steps.

1. Have couples prepare a list of compliments, validations, and supportive and loving statements that fit with the facts about their respective partner.
2. Next, have couples practice saying five of these kinds of statements to their partner before bringing up a complaint or something that has been bothering them.
3. Follow this with having couples practice this at home until it becomes more natural and easy to do.
4. Then have couples use the method the next time they have a conflict.
5. Follow up and adjust and coach as necessary.

This method can be used by your clients in any relationship (work, parenting, friends, family, and so on). If clients have conflictual or difficult relationships, have them try this method in any of those relationships and let you know what effects it has.

- Here are some examples of:
  - Validations:
    - "I know you have been working really hard lately."
    - "I have a sense you are really frustrated with me and the situation right now."

- Compliments:
    - "You have been putting a lot of effort into this relationship."
    - "You work really hard."
    - "I really like the way you think about what you are going to say before you say it."
    - "I have noticed that you are coming home earlier from work, as you said you would."

You can get more examples of "positives" from the couple and learn what kinds of statements (and nonverbal clues) seem helpful and supportive to each of them.

Reference

Allen, E. S., Rhoades, G. K., Stanley, S. M., Markman, H. J., Williams, T., Melton, J., & Clements, M. L. (2008). Premarital precursors of marital infidelity. *Family Process*, *47*(2), 243–259.
Gottman, J., Gottman, J., & DeClaire, J. (2006). *10 lessons to transform your marriage*. New York: Crown.

Additional Resource

O'Hanlon, B., & Hudson, P. (1994). *Love is a verb*. New York: W. W. Norton.

Getting to Know You

Overview

One of the greatest challenges in meeting new people and making new connections lies in extending ourselves in ways that may at times feel uncomfortable. Some of us are shy. Others are worried about being judged. And still others wonder if people will actually like them. The purpose of this exercise is twofold: to help clients (1) increase their comfort with getting to know others, and (2) create a foundation for strong relationships through better understanding of others' worlds. In his work with couples, psychologist John Gottman (1999) has referred to having genuine interest in and knowledge of a partner's world as developing a "cognitive room."

Suggestions for Use

This exercise can be especially useful for those clients who struggle with conversation starters and in meeting others. The basis of the exercise is for clients to not just connect with new people, but to form strong and enduring relationships. People who know what is important to others within their social networks tend to have more stable and satisfying relationships. This exercise will help clients get to know others in relatively innocuous but nonetheless very meaningful ways.

Exercise

To complete this exercise, have the client complete the following steps.

1. Make a list of the persons with whom you are closest in your life.

    _____   _____

    _____   _____

    _____   _____

    _____   _____

    _____   _____

    _____   _____

2. As you look over the list of names in Step 1, ask yourself, "How much do I really know about each of these people?" For example, do you know what kind of music they like? How about food? Do you know how each person would choose to take a vacation?

    Now, if you had trouble answering the previous questions, meet up with the person or persons in your list and learn more about them. Here are some questions you might consider asking:
    • What is your favorite food?
    • What is your favorite song (or CD or artist)?
    • Who is one person, dead or alive, you really admire? What do you most admire about that person?
    • What is your favorite season?
    • What is one moment you will never forget?
    • What makes you laugh?
    • Who is your favorite actor?
    • What is your favorite movie (or top five movies)?

- What is something you have read lately that you thoroughly enjoyed?
- What sports or hobbies do you enjoy?
- What is one place you have never been to visit during your lifetime?

There are many, many questions you could choose to ask. Be creative by making up your own. The point is to really get to know others and what is important to them. Knowing about others and what they value and find important is the basis for strong relationships. You may also find that when you ask others about their lives, the conversations will become rich and exciting. You will surely learn something you didn't know about someone if you take the time to ask.

3. After you have learned more about a person or persons in your life, write about what stood out for you with the experience.

_____

_____

_____

_____

_____

_____

4. This part of the exercise offers a way of extending yourself even further. Meet someone you don't know well or at all—at work, school, at a coffee shop, or elsewhere. Strike up a conversation and ask a few of the questions listed in Step 2 or use a few of your own. Then write about your experience in the space below.

_____

_____

_____

_____

_____

_____

Even if the person or persons you get to know do not become ongoing friends of yours or part of your social network, you will have done something very special for another person. You will have made an investment in another person and put him (her) front and center of your conversation.

Reference

Gottman, J. M. (1999). *The marriage clinic: A scientifically based marital therapy.* New York: W. W. Norton.

Stretch Yourself, Keep Expanding

Overview

This exercise focuses on a main pillar of Positive Psychology, that of positive relationships. It is an extension of the exercise "Connections" in Chapter 4. Because relationships and connection to others are essential to well-being and happiness, it is important to encourage clients to continue to expand their social networks and support systems. The purpose of this exercise is to help clients expand their already-existing social networks.

Suggestions for Use

This exercise can be helpful to all clients; however, it is recommended that clients first complete the exercise, "Connections" in Chapter 4. The focus of the exercise here is to help clients stretch or extend themselves beyond their current relationships to increase their social networks (O'Hanlon, 2000). It is recommended that clients be eased into this exercise as some will express uneasiness about venturing beyond their zones of comfort. Talk with clients about the small steps they can take, gradually suggesting slightly more adventurous steps as clients become more comfortable and experience success. It can also be helpful to pair this exercise with "Getting to Know You."

Exercise

To complete this exercise, have the client complete the following steps.

1. Think about the places you typically go and are comfortable hanging out. In the left-hand column, write the names of places you frequent with persons who are part of your social network. In the right-hand column, write the names of places you more often go by yourself. You may have some overlap between the two columns.

_____   _____

_____   _____

_____   _____

_____   _____

_____   _____

2. Next, as you look at the column on the left, consider how you might change some aspect or component related to the places you meet with others, how you meet, when you meet, and so on. For example, if you always meet your best friend for lunch on Saturdays at the same restaurant, try a different restaurant. Or, change what you usually eat or the time you usually meet. You might even talk with the person or persons with whom you meet regularly and plan a spontaneous change (e.g., agree to drive to a different section of town and go to a new restaurant, etc.). In the space below, write a few things you might do differently to stretch yourself just a little in this area.

_____

_____

_____

_____

_____

After trying something different, write about your experience with making that change.

_____

_____

_____

_____

_____

_____

_____

3. Now refer to the right-hand column under Step 1. Think about the places that you have considered going by yourself that are not on your list—but could be soon! First, make a list of those places in the space below. Don't hedge here! Be creative. You don't need to commit to going to all the places on your list.

_____

_____

_____

_____

_____

_____

_____

- What is most appealing about the places you listed?
- What would it take to get yourself to visit one of the places on your list?
- How might doing something to stretch yourself a little benefit you?

4. Make a plan to go during the next week to one of the places you listed under Step 3. Write about your experience in the space provided below. Be sure to speak about anything interesting that happened, including positive emotions or new connections.

_____

_____

_____

_____

_____

_____

_____

Reference

O'Hanlon, B. (2000). *Do one thing different*. New York: W. W. Norton.

Connections

Overview

One of the main pillars of Positive Psychology is positive relationships. Relationships and connections to others are essential to well-being and happiness. They provide support and opportunities to share experiences with others, and contribute to new meaning. The purpose of this exercise is to help clients identify past, present, or potential future connections that can enhance their lives. It is important to note that it is not the number of social connections people have, but rather the strength of those relationships. For some people, a single relationship can be more fulfilling than a dozen.

Suggestions for Use

This exercise can be helpful to all clients, but particularly to those who tend to restrict themselves relationally. That is, they do not routinely and consistently connect with others. This exercise can also be useful with those clients who isolate themselves when experiencing problems. For this exercise, first help clients identify those persons who they could connect or reconnect with. Next, help clients create a plan to increase the degree of social connection in their lives at least minimally.

Exercise

To complete this exercise, have the client complete the following steps.

1. Think about the role that relationships currently play in your life. Consider the following questions:
   - How many people would you say you maintain some routine and consistent connection with?
   - On average, how many social contacts do you have a month (i.e., face to face or on the phone for more than just five or so minutes) outside of work or school?
   - What has been the benefit of keeping in contact with others on a consistent basis?

   It is not the number of people that we know or consider connections, but rather how often we actually have quality contact with those persons in our social network. Examples might include going to lunch or a movie, being part of a book club, playing cards once a week, or chatting on the phone for 20 minutes to catch up. Whether our social network includes one person or 20 is less important than the time we spend with those we are close to and the level of support we provide each other within those relationships.

   Please review Figure 4.1. Placing yourself at the center, think about the people who might fit into your "Spoke of Life."

2. Next, make a list of those persons who fit into your current "Spokes of Life" and write their names in the space below. You may have more than person for each spoke or leave a spoke blank if it is not currently applicable to you. Remember that it is the not the number of people in your life but rather the quality of your connection to those persons. Having one person you can count on and who supports you is a great place to begin.

   _____   _____

   _____   _____

   _____   _____

   _____   _____

   _____   _____

FIGURE 4.1 The spokes of life.

3. Now think about how you might connect with one or more of the persons you listed under Step 2. Make a plan to minimally increase your connection to that person or persons. Write your plan in the space below.

_____

_____

_____

_____

_____

4. Write or talk with your therapist about your experience with increasing your connection to others.
5. Consider ways that you might meet new people or reconnect with others in the near future to expand your current social support system. If applicable, you might also talk with your therapist about ways to do this. It is also recommended that you complete the exercises "Stretch Yourself, Keep Expanding" and "Getting to Know You."

Resources

Bertolino, B. (2010). *Strengths-based engagement and practice: Creating effective helping relationships.* Boston, MA: Allyn & Bacon.

Bertolino, B., Kiener, M. S., & Patterson, R. (2009). *The therapist's notebook for strengths and solution-based therapies: Homework, handouts, and activities.* New York: Routledge/Taylor & Francis.

Cacioppo, J., & Patrick, W. (2008). *Loneliness: Human nature and the need for social connection.* New York: W.W. Norton.

Putnam, R. (2000). *Bowling alone: The collapse and revival of American community.* New York: Simon & Schuster.

Encouragements versus Discouragements

Overview

Similar to the positives-to-negatives ratio discussed in the previous section, there is interesting research about the difference between encouragements versus discouragements in the development and success of children. Researchers (Hart & Risley, 1995) studied children whose parents were on welfare versus those who were "middle class." They called these "disadvantaged" versus "advantaged" families, respectively. They discovered great disparity in the amount and type of parental talk to infants between disadvantaged families and those who had higher incomes and education.

Disadvantaged parents generally talked less to their children than advantaged parents (10 million words versus 80 million words, respectively). Disadvantaged parents directed more "discouragements" (e.g., no; shut up; stop) toward their kids (200,000 versus 80,000 "encouragements" [e.g., chit-chat, positive comments, gossip, joking, running commentary, praise]). Advantaged parents had a reversal of this ratio (500,000 encouragements to 80,000 discouragements). It turns out that these differences have profound and hard-to-reverse effects on intellectual and academic achievement (vocabulary growth and standardized intellectual achievement tests measured at ages 3 and 9). The purpose of this exercise is to help clients with encouragements among families.

Suggestions for Use

This research speaks to the importance of actually having whole families in one's office. In this direct observation situation, the therapist can get a sense of the ratio of encouragements to discouragements in a particular family. Then, using solution-based methods, one can evoke or discover things the parents can complement or encourage their children about.

Exercise

For this exercise, explore the following points with clients, preferably in the context of therapy.

- Catch parents doing any verbal and nonverbal encouragements they are doing and encourage them to do more of that.
- If appropriate, tell them about the research cited above and enlist their cooperation in shifting the ratio of encouragements to discouragements in a good direction.
- Then have them practice this at home until it becomes more natural and easy to do.
- Follow up and adjust and coach as necessary.

This method can be used by your clients in any relationship (work, parenting, friends, family, and so on). If clients have conflictual or difficult relationships, have them try this method in any of those relationships and let you know what effects it has.

Reference

Hart, B., & Risley, T. (1995). *Meaningful differences in the everyday experience of young American children.* Baltimore, MD: Paul H. Brookes Publishing Company.

Two Pathways to Social Connection

Overview

In this section we discuss the two types of social connections that have been shown to help increase happiness and well-being and help prevent problems. The first is one-to-one relationships. Philosopher Martin Buber (1947/2002) called this type of social connection the I–Thou relationship, in which real connection occurs (as opposed to the I–It relationship, in which people objectify each other or don't have an authentic encounter, dialogue, and connection).

This type of connection includes

- Friendships
- Pets
- Marriage
- Intimate partnerships
- Child–parent relationships

As you can see, many of these are human-to-human relationships, but ones with pets can also be significant social connections. Many isolated people feel socially connected to their pets and sometimes through their pets, they connect to other humans (just take a dog for a walk in a park to see this phenomenon at work).

The other type of social connection is with groups of people. Humans evolved in groups and tribes and seem to thrive in larger social groups. When one hears about someone who shot up a workplace or school, one often hears afterward that "He was a loner," and this is not surprising. Social connections hold people in check and give them reasons for not doing harm to others (Cacioppo & Patrick, 2008).

This kind of connection includes

- Neighborhoods
- Interest groups
- Church communities
- Professional or work groups
- Groups of friends
- Sports teams
- Military units
- Support groups
- Book groups
- Sewing or quilting circles
- Musical groups/choirs
- Political or social action groups
- Extended family
- Nuclear family

These days, people can find connections in social media groups such as Facebook. This exercise can help to further encourage connections.

Suggestions for Use

Given the importance of social connections, it would be wise to do a social connection inventory with clients to determine the extent of their connection or isolation. If relevant, you could encourage your client to do a social connection tune-up, making an effort to move against the tendency of our busy, modern lives to become isolated and disconnected from one another.

Exercise

For this exercise, explore the following areas with clients.

Social Connection Inventory

- Do you have any close relationships? Y/N
  - A close or best friend? Y/N
  - A close colleague at work? Y/N
  - An intimate/romantic relationship? Y/N
- Do you have a pet (or more than one)? Y/N
  - If yes, does this pet help you feel connected? Y/N
- Do you have a relationship with your family of origin?
  - Are you close with either or both of your parents? Y/N
  - Are you close or do you feel connected with any or all or your siblings? Y/N
- Do you have children? Y/N
  - If yes, are you close or connected with that child or those children? Y/N
- Do you belong to any clubs or social groups? Y/N
- Do you regularly get together with a group of friends? Y/N
- Do you belong to any religious congregation or community? Y/N
  - If so, do you attend services or activities in that community regularly? Y/N
  - Do you feel connected to this community? Y/N
- Do you feel part of your workgroup? Y/N
  - Do you have a particular close friend at work? Y/N
  - Do you do things outside work hours with people from work? Y/N
- Do you play sports or belong to any sports team? Y/N
  - Do you play regularly? Y/N
- Do you belong to a military unit or veterans group? Y/N
  - If so, do you stay in touch with this group? Y/N
- Do you know and interact socially with your neighbors? Y/N
- Do you play or sing in some musical group? Y/N
  - Do you regularly attend those/that group? Y/N
- Do you do any arts or crafts activities with groups? Y/N
  - Do you regularly attend those/that group? Y/N
- Do you belong to any support groups?
  - Do you regularly attend those/that group? Y/N
- Is there any social connection that you would like to strengthen or renew? Y/N
- If so, what and how?

References

Buber, M. (1947/2002). *Between man and man.* New York: Routledge.

Cacioppo, J., & Patrick, W. (2008). *Loneliness: Human nature and the need for social connection.* New York: W.W. Norton.

Safety in Numbers

Overview

In Chapter 4 of this book we discussed how family rituals could have a preventative effect for many troubles. Having good social relationships is correlated with higher levels of happiness and well-being. And, there is some evidence that being in social situations seems to guard against PTSD (post-traumatic stress disorder) and help one recover at a higher rate from PTSD.

A study of survivors of an earthquake in Armenia found that being with someone else during an earthquake is protective against PTSD (Armenian et al., 2000). Another study found that PTSD sufferers in group treatment recovered at a significantly higher rate (88.3%) than those in individual treatment (31.3%) (Beck et al., 2009).

Robert Biswas-Diener and Ed Diener (2001) surveyed life satisfaction of the homeless and prostitutes living in the slums of Calcutta and found that healthy bonds with family and good social relationships were correlated with higher life satisfaction levels. Those without such protective factors had much lower rates of life satisfaction and well-being levels.

Bill had a client who was feeling isolated after a traumatic divorce in which she temporarily lost custody of her children due to her ex-husband's manipulation of the court system. As the U.S. holiday of Thanksgiving approached, her ex promised her that their youngest child could spend the holiday with her in her new apartment, but at the last minute he reneged. There she was, in an almost empty apartment, not knowing a soul, with a defrosted turkey and all the holiday fixings, and facing a depressing day. She suddenly thought of going around to the doors of neighbors she hadn't met (it was a new apartment complex and many people had just recently moved in) and inviting them to share her dinner. She got no response at the first door on which she knocked. At the second one, the woman looked at her like she was crazy when she explained her situation and offered her invitation. She almost gave up, but then remembered something she had heard about newcomers to AA, the alcoholic recovery self-help group. When people go to their first AA meeting, they are often feeling alienated and different or frightened, and never return for a second meeting. The advice they are given is to go to three meetings, no matter how they feel and then decide, but not before three tries. My client decided she would go to the third door. There she met a delightful couple who did not have any plans or even enough money to buy a turkey and they were happy to join her. They went with her to several more doors and it turned into a nice gathering in which five neighbors shared a holiday dinner and got to know one another. What could have been a depressing day turned into a day of social connection and budding friendship.

Suggestions for Use

One of the things that is common among sufferers of problems like PTSD and depression is that the sufferer often becomes more isolated, in part because he feels that others can't understand his situation, or he feels himself a burden to others. Or, it might be that his behavior is challenging or offputting to others.

Whatever the cause, it appears that helping people become reconnected socially can be helpful in both the prevention of further problems and recovery from current problems.

Self-help and support groups, group therapy, and online communities of like-minded people or people with similar interests can be one path to social reconnection. Approaching friends or family from whom the person has been distant is another path to social reconnection. Be attentive to reports or opportunities for the client to make positive social connections and encourage and support those when possible.

Exercise

For this exercise, as a therapist, complete the following steps.

- Ask clients where they have good social connections.
- Explore where they may have drifted away from good social connections and investigate whether or not they could renew or strengthen some of those social relationships.
- Encourage isolated clients to find like-minded people or support groups.
- Start a group for clients with similar issues.

References

Armenian, H. et al. (2000). Loss as a determinant of PTSD in a cohort of adult survivors of the 1998 earthquake in Armenia: Implications for policy. *Acta Psychiatrica Scandinavica, 102*(1), 58–64.

Beck, J. G., Coffey, S. F., Foy, D. W., Keane, T., & Blanchard, E. B. (2009). Group cognitive behavior therapy for chronic posttraumatic stress disorder: An initial randomized pilot study. *Behavior Therapy*, *40*(1), 82–92.

Biswas-Diener, R., & Diener, E. (2001). Making the best of a bad situation: Satisfaction in the slums of Calcutta. *Social Indicators Research*, *55*, 329–352.

Like Benjamin Button

Overview

In the short story by F. Scott Fitzgerald and subsequent motion picture, "The Curious Case of Benjamin Button," a child is born with the body of an elderly man. Over time, Benjamin grows younger and younger physically until he becomes an infant. One of the lessons of the story is how we can continue to be curious about the world and never stop learning. In fact, research suggests (Medina, 2009) that engaging in meaningful activities that stimulate intellectual functioning can slow the progression of mental decline in the later years of life. The purpose of this exercise is to help clients maintain their curiosity as they get older and engage in meaningful learning experiences.

Suggestions for Use

Zen Master Shunryu Suzuki (Suzuki, 1973) once said, "In the beginner's mind there are many possibilities, in the expert's mind there are few." This exercise involves helping clients maintain their sense of curiosity about learning throughout life. There are many ways to vary this exercise to fit clients. In this case we present the exercise in a general form that can be applied with clients of different ages and life experiences. The main focus is to encourage "a life well-lived." In the same vein, the benefits for a beginner's or "young mind" are numerous—creativity, spontaneity, healthier immune system, and so on.

Note: In using this exercise, it may be helpful, but not required, to have clients watch the film, *The Curious Case of Benjamin Button* (Paramount, 2008). You might also discuss the movie with your client prior to beginning the exercise.

Exercise

To complete the following exercise, have the client complete the following steps.

1. Begin by reading the following quote:
   "In the beginner's mind there are many possibilities, in the expert's mind there are few."
   • What comes to mind when you reflect on the quote?

   _____

   _____

   _____

   _____

   _____

2. Comprise a brief list of things that you understand very well or can do very well (e.g., mathematics, car repair, cooking, philosophy, etc.) by your own standards. Write your responses in the column on the left.

   _____   _____

   _____   _____

   _____   _____

   _____   _____

   _____   _____

   _____   _____

3. Review your list from Step 2. For each item you placed in the left-hand column, write one thing you can do that would advance your knowledge of that item. Be creative and consider those things that will pique your curiosity, even if it means challenging what you already know.

_____

_____

_____

_____

_____

_____

_____

_____

_____

_____

4. Make a plan to follow through with one or more of the things you will do to advance your knowledge or improve on an already-existing skill. Be specific about your plan, including your time frame for engaging in the activity. Write about your plan in the space provided below.

_____

_____

_____

_____

_____

_____

_____

_____

_____

_____

5. To further practice your beginner's mind, make a commitment to do one of the following things:
   - Take a class that moves you to a different level of knowledge or ability about a subject you already have some knowledge about or skill in.
   - Learn about a historical figure who you know little or nothing about.
   - Try to solve a puzzle or problem that is new to you.
   - Study a problem or situation from at least three different perspectives.
   - Talk with someone who you know little about and ask that person to tell you about his (her) life story.
   - Learn about a culture that differs from yours.
   - Listen to a kind of music that you are unfamiliar with or read something that is outside the kind of reading you typically do.
   - Go someplace you have never been and immerse yourself in the experience of that new place.

6. Write about your experience with Step 4 or 5. Be sure to talk about what you learned that was new and what that experience meant to you.

_____

_____

_____

_____

_____

_____

_____

_____

_____

_____

_____

References

Medina, J. (2009). *Brain rules: 12 principles for surviving and thriving at work, home, and school.* Seattle, WA: Pear Press.

Suzuki, S. (1973). *Zen mind, beginner's mind.* New York: Weatherhill [now Shambhala].

Spread the Word

Overview

Some people read nonfiction; others prefer spy or mystery novels or poetry. No matter the kind of literature, written words can help people feel better and change their perspective on things. In some cases, literature can inspire people to change their lives. The purpose of this exercise is to identify books that have been meaningful and then share them with others. In short, this exercise is about the gift of giving.

Suggestions for Use

This exercise is best suited for people who enjoy reading. The premise of this exercise is to encourage clients to pass along the readings they have most enjoyed, found inspiration in, and have perhaps led to a change in their lives. The passing along of favorite readings does several things: It allows others to enjoy readings that others have found helpful, it serves as a gift from one person to another, it connects people in new ways, and it is economical. There are of course other benefits too that are to be discovered by those who engage in the exercise!

Exercise

Bob has a good friend, Jeff, with whom for many years he has seen countless movies and discussed the latest literary musings. Jeff has a particular ritual that has now reached hundreds of people. When Jeff reads a book, he writes his name and his phone number in it. Then he passes it along to another person. Books Jeff has read have now reached hundreds of people and touched their lives. Jeff has been contacted by people he has never met and thanked them for passing along a book. In essence, Jeff's gift to others continues to touch lives in ways he never imagined.

To complete this exercise, follow each of the steps that follow.

1. Make a list of your favorite books and write the names of them in the space below.

---

2. Put a checkmark next to the books you have copies of that you would be willing to pass along to others. For those books that you do not have copies of or would rather not part with, consider purchasing extra copies from a local bookseller or through the Internet. You may also consider finding used books online. Oftentimes, books can be found at heavily discounted rates.

3. For those books that you are willing to part with or have extra copies of, write your name in the top left-hand corner of an inner page of each book. Then write, "Please pass this book along when you are done with it." You might also leave a very brief note such as, "This book changed my life" or "May you find joy in these pages." Finally, if you are comfortable, include a phone number or e-mail address. Then give the book away. You are now spreading the word!

Note: This exercise can also be done with articles, poems, or other forms of the written word. Please be sure to abide by all applicable copyright laws.

Note: There is an online version of this practice. Visit www.goodreads.com and consider becoming part of social community of readers and recommendations.

Have You Heard?

Overview

There is a fondness among some for repeating famous (or not so famous, in some cases) quotes, poems, lyrics to songs, or lines from movies. Although favorite sayings are often used for humor or to make a point, many sayings also provide meaning for those who use them. Some are, in fact, sources of inspiration. The purpose of this exercise is to both identify favorite quotes, lines, lyrics, or sayings and share them with others to make them laugh, feel better, smile, express gratitude, or simply let them know you care.

Suggestions for Use

This exercise can be used with all clients. It's also an example of an exercise that can provide an immediate boost to happiness by making people laugh and have them share positive experiences. It is noteworthy that sometimes people will struggle with this exercise. They may not read much, listen to music, or watch movies. In such cases, clients can be asked to think about quotes they have heard from others that have stuck with them or are meaningful to them. For others, it might be easier to have them think of a single line from a song that evokes a sense of happiness or peace.

Exercise

For this exercise, have the client complete the following steps.

1. Think of a favorite you have for each of the areas below. If you can't think of anything for a given area, just take a pass and come back to it later if you wish.
   • Favorite Quote:

   _____
   _____
   _____
   _____
   _____

   • Favorite Song Lyric:

   _____
   _____
   _____
   _____
   _____

   • Favorite Movie Line/Quote:

   _____
   _____
   _____
   _____
   _____

• Favorite Poem/Passage from Book:

_____
_____
_____
_____
_____

• Favorite "Off-the-Cuff" Saying Phrase (e.g., "It is what it is," "Wherever I go, there you are," etc.):

_____
_____
_____
_____
_____

2. Select one of your favorites—ideally one that is meaningful for you in some way. Next, consider the following questions:
   • What is it about the particular quote, line, passage, or saying that really resonates with you?
   • How has it been helpful to you to refer back to it from time to time?
3. Share your favorites with another person and talk about the meanings your favorites have for each of you.

You Say You're Stubborn, I Say Determined

Overview

One of the things we have been very careful about in translating Positive Psychology research into clinical applications is to remain realistic. We don't want to delude ourselves or our clients by wearing "rose-colored glasses" in the face of their very real and palpable suffering and problems. But it turns out that there is some research that shows that having what are called "positive illusions" about one's spouse or partner can increase satisfaction in relationships.

Sandra Murray and colleagues at SUNY Buffalo have done many research studies (Murray & Holmes, 1993; Murray, Holmes, & Griffin, 1996; Murray, Holmes, Dolderman, & Griffin, 2000) in which they have found that if one sees one's partner more positively than they see themselves, the relationship is better (rated more positively and satisfying). Also, it helps to reframe their negative qualities as assets.

Suggestions for Use

This exercise is primarily for clients in close romantic/sexual relationships. Inspired by this research, the therapist can help clients begin to transform their views of their spouses or partners by reframing what they or others may see as their partner's flaws into admirable traits.

Exercise

Explain to the couples the research that shows that people who see their partners in the most positive light are happier and more satisfied than those who don't.

* Have each partner make a list of flaws or foibles their partner may have. These may come from the partner's own self-criticism (e.g., "I'm such a klutz," or "I can't stay organized.") or it may come from their partner or others (e.g., "She's controlling," or "He's always late.").
* Have them spend a little time considering how this trait or flaw could be an asset and something admirable (e.g., "She's controlling" could become "She knows what she wants and goes after it."; "He's always late" can become "He's a free spirit who lives in the moment.").
* Have each partner write these down and carry them around for a month. Every time someone says something about a negative or problematic trait, have the partner transform those critiques or negatives judgments into these "positive illusions."
* Check in with the couple at the end of the month to discover how things have shifted and if they would like to continue to use this method.

References

Murray, S. L., & Holmes, J. G. (1993). Seeing virtues in faults: Negativity and the transformation of interpersonal narratives in close relationships. *Journal of Personality and Social Psychology*, *65*, 707–722.

Murray, S. L., Holmes, J. G., Dolderman, D., & Griffin, D. W. (2000). What the motivated mind sees: Comparing friends' perspectives to married partners' views of each other. *Journal of Experimental Social Psychology*, *36*, 600–620.

Murray, S. L., Holmes, J. G., & Griffin, D. W. (1996). The benefits of positive illusions: Idealization and the construction of satisfaction in close relationships. *Journal of Personality and Social Psychology Bulletin*, *70*, 79–98.

Rituals of Connection and Continuity

Overview

A review (Fiese et al., 2002) of 50 years of research (32 studies) on family rituals showed that regular routines had a positive effect on health and family relationships. Common routines included dinnertime rituals, bedtime rituals, daily or weekly chores, talking regularly on the phone with family members, visiting relatives, birthday celebrations, holidays together, family reunions, funerals, and religious rituals and services.

Rituals of connection and continuity are regularly repeated, nonharmful activities that people do together. These rituals help people connect to others and have a sense of stability over time. Modern society makes it challenging to keep these rituals going. Therapists can investigate, discover, and encourage such rituals to enhance people's social connections.

In another study (Ivanova & Israel, 2005), researchers talked to current college students and measured their family of origin's level of comforting and safe rituals, and discovered there was a correlation between the amount of those rituals and the student's current level of depression (that is, fewer childhood rituals were correlated with higher depression levels).

A study (QEV Analytics, 2003) reported by the Center on Addiction and Substance Abuse (housed at Columbia University) found that kids who have regular family mealtimes are at lower risk for suicidal thoughts and are more likely to do better in school. Teens who have regular family dinners were more likely to be emotionally content, to work harder and do better in school, to have good peer relationships, and to have better eating habits. They also found that adolescents who have family meals had lower stress and reported less boredom. Bored teens are 50% more likely than teens who are not often bored to smoke, drink, get drunk, and use illegal drugs.

Suggestions for Use

Ask some simple questions about current rituals in the client's and the client's family life. Ask in some detail about the nature of those rituals and their regularity. Discover if there were some rituals that used to happen but have dropped away or been disrupted in the recent past.

Exercise

For this exercise, use the following areas of focus with clients.

- Encourage clients, couples, and families to develop mutual and nonharmful rituals of connection and continuity.
- These can also be individual, not just social rituals. Things like taking a walk daily, writing in a journal, praying, meditating, and reading can help the person reduce stress levels and create a sense of stability in a busy, stressed, and chaotic life.
- Check in with them to find out the effects and whether they are sticking with the rituals.
- Follow up and adjust and coach as necessary.

References

Fiese, B. H., Tomcho, T. J., Douglas, M., Josephs, K., Poltrock, S., & Baker, T. (2002). A review of 50 years of research on naturally occurring family routines and rituals: Cause for celebration? *Journal of Family Psychology, 16*(4), 381–390.

Ivanova, M., & Israel, A. (2005). Family stability as a protective factor against the influences of pessimistic attributional style on depression. *Cognitive Therapy and Research, 29*(2), 243–251.

Additional Resources

Bennett, L., Wolin, S., Reiss, D., & Teitelbaum, M. (1987). Couples at risk for transmission of alcoholism: Protective influences. *Family Process, 2,* 111–129.

Imber-Black, E., Roberts, J., & Whiting, R. (1988). *Rituals in families and family therapy.* New York: W. W. Norton.

Markson, S, & Fiese, B. (2000). Family rituals as a protective factor for children with asthma. *Journal of Pediatric Psychology, 25,* 471–479.

QEV Analytics. (2003). *The importance of family dinners.* Retrieved from Casacolumbia.org.

Van der Hart, O. (1983). *Rituals in psychotherapy: Transition and continuity.* New York: Irvington.

Wolin, S. J., & Bennett, L. A. (1984). Family rituals. *Family Process, 23,* 401–420.

Plan for It

Overview

When people get busy, one of the first things that "goes by the wayside" is social connections. In fact, research has shown that the number of social connections people have each month has decreased significantly over the past two decades (Putnam, 2000). It's not that people don't want to spend time together, it's just that they see social relationships as static—that they are always going to be there. But all relationships take time and effort. The purpose of this exercise is to build relational "muscles" through deliberate planning and action.

Suggestions for Use

This exercise requires that clients get involved in planning an activity or event and following through with those plans. To prepare clients for this activity, be sure to talk about the importance of social connections to their lives. Sometimes it can be helpful to discuss how it can be difficult in the midst of busy schedules to get together with others but how the value of those get-togethers can extend way beyond the activity or event itself. From there, suggest that the client put some thought into an activity or event that he (she) could arrange to connect with people in his (her) life.

Exercise

For this activity, have the client complete the following steps.

1. Think of an activity or event that would bring you and others together in a meaningful way. The activity should be something that can be planned and carried out within a brief period of time (i.e., no longer than a month from the development of the plan). The activity should be fun, created with respect to cost, and involve at least three persons.

    Give a brief description of the activity and the steps you will take to make it happen. Keep the number of steps to five or less.

_____

_____

_____

_____

_____

_____

_____

_____

_____

Steps:

1. _____

2. _____

3. _____

4. _____

5. _____

2. Write about your experience of doing the activity. Specifically, what stood out for you? What difference did the activity make for you? For others?

_____

_____

_____

_____

_____

_____

_____

_____

_____

_____

3. Invite other people who were present to each take a turn planning an event in the future!

Reference

Putnam, R. (2000). *Bowling alone: The collapse and revival of American community.* New York: Simon & Schuster.

Increase Gratitude and Appreciation

"The aim of life is appreciation." –G.K. Chesterton

This chapter is about awe, gratitude, and profound appreciation. These moments come rarely in life and are usually treasured when they arrive. And why do they arrive so rarely? Well, our brains seem to be built that way. Once we get used to seeing or experiencing something, it drops out of our awareness. It is probably more efficient for our brains to do this and to attend to novel things in our environments. These could be threats or new sources of food.

Dan Gilbert (2006), in speaking about this human tendency, writes:

> When we have an experience—hearing a particular sonata, making love with a particular person, watching the sun set from a particular window of a particular room—on successive occasions, we quickly begin to adapt to it, and the experience yields less pleasure each time. Psychologists call this habituation, economists call it declining marginal utility, and the rest of us call it marriage. (p. 130)

This human tendency is why we notice that beautiful sunset the first few days of our island vacation but often ignore it after two weeks. It's why we are thrilled with our new car the first several days, weeks, or months, but then the thrill abates. It's why when we are ill or injured, we vow we will never take walking, talking, or feeling good for granted again, but then quickly take those things for granted when they return. It's why we take our romantic partners for granted as well, even though when we first met them, the sound of their voice and their lightest touch could send us into ecstasy.

There is substantial evidence that gratitude and appreciation can affect happiness levels and even give people some traction out of serious depression. Expressing gratitude has a short-term positive effect (several weeks) on happiness levels (up to a 25% increase). Those who are typically or habitually grateful are happier than those who aren't habitually grateful (Park, Peterson, & Seligman, 2004).

In another study (Emmons & McCullough, 2003), 100+ adults were asked to keep a journal and were randomly assigned to three different groups:

> Group A wrote about things about which they felt grateful;
> Group B wrote about things they found annoying or irritating; and
> Group C wrote about things that had had a major impact on them.

Two out of the three different experiments were relatively intense and short term (keeping a daily journal for two to three weeks), while one required a weekly entry during 10 weeks.

People in the gratitude group generally evidenced higher levels of well-being than those in the comparison conditions, especially when compared to Group B (the one journaling about hassles), but also compared to the "neutral" group.

In the longer study, which ran for 10 weeks, there was a positive effect on hours of sleep and on time spent exercising, on more optimistic expectations for the coming week, and fewer reported physical symptoms, such as pain, as well as an increase in reported connectedness to other people and a likelihood of helping another person deal with a personal problem.

Another study was done by Martin Seligman and Jeff Levy (cited in Seligman, 2002) with people who scored as severely depressed in a depression inventory. Participants were instructed to recall and write three good things that happened each day for 15 days. Some 94% of them went from severely depressed to mildly or moderately depressed during that time. This chapter, then, is about some things one can deliberately do in life to recapture and rekindle this sense of awe, appreciation, and gratitude.

References

Emmons, R., & McCullough, M. (2003). Counting blessings versus burdens: An experimental investigation of gratitude and subjective well-being in daily life. *Journal of Personality and Social Psychology, 84*(2), 377–389.

Gilbert, D. (2006). *Stumbling on happiness*. New York: Knopf.

Park, N., Peterson, C., & Seligman, M. (2004). *Strengths of character and well-being among youth*. Unpublished manuscript, University of Rhode Island.

Seligman, M. (2002). *Authentic happiness*. New York: Free Press.

The Three Types of Savoring

Overview

One aspect of happiness and life satisfaction is savoring. According to the *American Heritage Dictionary*, to savor is "to appreciate fully, enjoy or relish." Savoring involves paying full attention to something in one's experience. Savoring also involves engaging in the experience. Too many times in our busy, multitasking life, we miss the actual experience we might be having. It is said that few people who visit the magnificent Grand Canyon in the American Southwest actually see it directly any longer. They only see it through the digital camera or video screen they have in front of their eyes so they can see later what they would have been seeing if they'd bothered to look.

Savoring is not equal to pleasure, but refers more to appreciating and noticing and engaging in some experience. One could even savor a bitter-tasting food, or a feeling of melancholy. The purpose of this exercise is for clients to more fully appreciate and pay full attention to their own experiences.

Bill used to run encounter groups and awareness groups in the early 1970s, and one of the typical exercises in those groups was to have people focus on sensory experiences and savor them without analyzing or overthinking. In one example, participants would put on blindfolds and a partner would put a cut strawberry on their tongue, followed by a slice of lemon, followed by a piece of chocolate. Recipients were to remain open and aware of the taste and sensations. And this really illustrates the essence of savoring. It is paying attention to the experience of the moment and an appreciation of that experience.

Here we introduce three types to savor one's experience.

The first and most common type of savoring is **Present-Oriented Savoring**, in which one is enjoying and engaging fully in some experience in the moment. Some activities one might do to experience present-oriented savoring include

- Cell phone-, e-mail-, TV-, computer-free time periods
- Sensory focus moments (using visual, auditory, kinesthetic, olfactory, or gustatory senses)
- Watching sunrise or sunset
- Feeling the breeze with eyes closed
- Smelling food or environmental scents
- Tuning in to bodily sensations
- Tasting/savoring food
- Slow eating with no distractions
- Mindfulness practices
- Tuning in to feelings of the moment

The next is **Past-Oriented Savoring**, in which we vividly recall something we experienced and treasured in the past. This type of savoring might also involve reliving or re-experiencing a significant experience by telling it to others. Some activities one might do to experience past-oriented savoring include

- Replaying happy days
- Keeping a savoring photo album
- Remembering acts of kindness
- Recalling best moments

Last is **Future-Oriented Savoring**, in which we anticipate something good we expect to or want to have happen in the future. These are essentially vivid, engaging daydreams. Some activities one might do to experience future-oriented savoring include

- Vividly imaging an anticipated event
- Imagining what the future without some current hassle or problem would be
- Exploring your best possible future-self
- Detailing the components of your ideal day

All three forms of savoring can significantly enhance one's experience of joy and satisfaction.

Suggestions for Use

Many of our clients have habits of "going unconscious," that is, not being present in their relationships or for the significant life experiences they are having. This can diminish their sense of happiness, life satisfaction, and well-being.

A simple field study (Bryant & Veroff, 2007) was done on the effect of savoring on happiness. Students at a university were divided into three groups and were instructed to take a daily 20-minute walk for the next week. One-third were instructed to notice as many positive things as they could (e.g., sunshine, flowers, music, and so on) and to acknowledge those things and identify what it is they enjoyed about them. One-third were asked to do the same thing but to notice things that annoyed them (e.g., litter, graffiti, noise, and so on). The last third was told to just go for a walk without any particular instructions. As might be expected, those students who savored the positive while on walks showed greater happiness levels after one week.

We can help clients rehabilitate their sense of satisfaction by helping them practice savoring these moments. We can guide them to practice savoring in sessions and suggest they use the same ability outside sessions.

Exercise

When clients are experiencing something significant, suggest that they stop for a moment and savor that experience. That is, to pay close attention to what they are experiencing, especially the sensory aspects. Are they feeling anything particular in a certain part of their body? Has the light in the room seemed to become different? Can they become aware of their feelings?

Suggest that clients practice savoring at home during significant moments. Remind them to

- Pay full attention; engage in the experience.
- Use as many of the senses as they can (sight, sound, touch, taste, smell).
- Don't multi-task; focus on what they are experiencing or perceiving.
- Don't overdo; savoring diminishes due to the adaptation if done too much or too often.

After trying one or more of the methods of savoring, have clients report back on his their experience. Write the essence of that experience in the space provided below.

_____
_____
_____
_____
_____

Reference

Bryant, F., & Veroff, J. (2007). *Savoring: A new model of positive experience.* Mahwah, NJ: Lawrence Erlbaum.

Additional Resources

Bryant, F., Smart, C., & King, S. (2005). Using the past to enhance the present: Boosting happiness through positive reminiscence. *Journal of Happiness Studies, 6,* 227–260.

Gable, S., Reis, H., Impett, E., & Asher, E. (2004). What do you do when things go right? The intrapersonal and interpersonal benefits of sharing positive events. *Journal of Personality and Social Psychology, 87,* 228–245.

Validation

Overview

Validation can be described as actions that espouse both appreciation and gratitude. In a general sense, validation is a form of acknowledgment that places others at the center of attention, letting them know they are valued and appreciated. This purpose of this exercise is for participants to better connect with validation by acknowledging others and letting them know they are important. Although the intent behind this exercise is to acknowledge others, it is clear that this kind of exercise has further positive "side effects" in that persons who convey validation very often experience a lift in their own sense of well-being. Validation can be a gift that keeps giving.

Suggestions for Use

This exercise involves the use of the short film *Validation* (2007), in which a parking attendant uses validation to help people feel more positive emotion and well-being. It is not necessary to view the film; however, doing so typically gives more meaning to the exercise as a whole. The film can be found on various Internet sites such as YouTube. It is also recommended that as a therapist, you preview the movie prior to suggesting it to a client. It is important to ensure that the exercise is a good fit for your client. If you plan to use the film as part of the exercise, be sure to make sure that the client has access to the Internet.

Exercise

To complete this exercise, first determine whether or not the short film *Validation* (2007) will be used. The film can be found on different Internet sites, including YouTube. The film is approximately 16 minutes in length so it is important to allot enough time. If the film is being used, proceed with the exercise from the beginning. If the film is not being used, then skip ahead in the exercise to Step 3.

1. Begin by watching the short film *Validation*. The film involves a parking attendant who uses validation to recognize others and help them experience positive emotion.
2. Immediately after watching the film, briefly describe your experience. In particular, what do you notice about how you feel? What thoughts do you have about the idea of validation?

_____

_____

_____

_____

_____

_____

3. Take a moment to consider a few of the aspects of validation. Validation
   • Is genuine and heartfelt.
   • Includes but isn't limited to friends and family members; is extended to total strangers and people who may never be seen again.
   • Goes beyond smiles, eye contact, and general comments such as "Good morning" or "Hello"; it involves a personalized statement with the aim of leaving the person with a

positive experience (e.g., "That is a beautiful hat," "You have an amazing smile," "You really light up a room when you enter it," etc.).

- Can be a compliment about something a person has done, the impact a person has had on the people around, or the attractiveness of something a person is wearing.

4. Think about the day you have planned for tomorrow. Where will you go (i.e., work, gas station, post office, the coffee shop, etc.)? Who might you encounter? How might you validate one or more persons? Write in the space below three things you can do the next day to validate at least three people. Even if your plans change and you go different places and encounter different people, having several ideas in mind will prepare you and keep you in the validating mind-set!

1. _____
2. _____
3. _____

5. At the end of your day, take a moment to reflect on your experience of extending validation to others. What did you notice? Write your reflections in the space below.

_____
_____
_____
_____
_____
_____
_____
_____
_____
_____
_____

Reference

Kuenne, K. (Writer/Director/Composer). (2007). *Validation.* USA: Independent short film.

List Negative Things That Are No Longer Happening

Overview

When we of a certain age who grew up in the United States were children, our parents occasionally said to us, "You should be grateful you have food; there are children starving in China." For later generations, Ethiopia was substituted for China. This was supposed to make us grateful for the food on our plates (and to eat things we didn't prefer). We suspect it rarely had the intended effect.

Our technique and exercise here is akin to this, but we hope it has a better effect. It involves asking people to think about struggles or circumstances that were previously very difficult but are no longer happening in the person's life as a way to appreciate their current circumstances.

Again, based on the way the brain works, once we get used to a certain circumstance, we don't really notice it. If we used to live in a cramped, damp apartment with noisy neighbors above, we longed for the day we owned our own nice house. But once we get that house, we begin to forget how bad that apartment was and how nice we have it now. This is called, in Positive Psychology, the hedonic treadmill (Gilbert, 2006). To jar ourselves out of this hedonic treadmill way of thinking or feeling, we can use the past and its troubles as a contrast to re-notice and appreciate the present. The purpose of this exercise is to help clients to do this very thing.

Suggestions for Use

This exercise can be helpful when you know the client has had some rough times or troubles in the past. It is used to enhance appreciation of what is in the person's life right now in a backward way, and thus can enhance happiness, satisfaction, and happiness.

Exercise

For this exercise, follow the sequence below and jot down any significant comments or remarks the client makes throughout the process.

- Have the client list some difficult times in the past, problems he (she) used to have, relationships that they or he/she are no longer in that were bad for him (her), or times of illness, injury, or disability that are now resolved and behind him (her).

  _____

  _____

  _____

  _____

  _____

- Ask the client to bring you back to those difficulties and tell you what was so hard about those situations and times. Then ask the client how he (she) got through them or left them behind.

  _____

  _____

  _____

  _____

  _____

- Ask the client about his (her) current life in relation to those troubles, problems, previous relationships, and illnesses, injuries, or disabilities.

_____

_____

_____

_____

_____

- After this discussion, ask clients to note how they are feeling and their sense of their current life.

_____

_____

_____

_____

_____

Reference

Gilbert, D. (2006). *Stumbling on happiness.* New York: Knopf.

I Just Wanted You to Know

Overview

One of the most significant contributors to well-being is the expression of gratitude. There are many ways to let others know that we appreciate them and what they do for us, others, our communities, and the world around us. This exercise involves a specific way that people can express gratitude through the written word. The purpose of this exercise is twofold: (1) to let others know that they are appreciated, and (2) for the client who completes the exercise to have a positive experience in expressing gratitude. The second purpose of the exercise is the most important as it can help clients to more deliberately connect with the experience of appreciation. This is a well-researched activity in the Positive Psychology literature and has been found to increase happiness levels in both the expresser and the receiver of the gratitude (Emmons, 2007; Peterson, 2006).

Suggestions for Use

This exercise is best for clients who could benefit from expressing themselves in written form. Clients can write letters, send e-mails, leave "post-it" notes, or use artwork for this exercise. In talking about this exercise, it might be better to have clients start small. It is not necessary to express gratitude to everyone at once, and small expressions can be as significant as lengthy detailed ones. What is crucial is that the client experience positive emotion around the exercise, regardless of whether or not his (her) expression is reciprocated. This exercise is about giving appreciation without expecting anything in return.

Exercise

Have the client make a list of persons whom he (she) wishes to express gratitude. To generate conversation, it may be helpful to suggest that the client think of small acts of kindness, direct or indirect. An example of a direct gesture could be a person who helped the client move into a new home. An example of an indirect gesture could be a customer service representative who helped the client with a billing matter. The list of persons need not be extensive, just a starting point. In many cases, once a couple of names are listed, others will come to mind for clients.

Next, have the client select one person from the list. Then have the client write a brief note that can be mailed, e-mailed, faxed, or delivered by the client person to person. To assist with this process, have the client include the parts listed below in the note. Space has been provided to encourage the client to create a draft of the note.

1. Name of the person who the client wishes to express gratitude to:

---

2. A brief statement of the act or action the intended receiver of the gratitude performed:

Example: On June 14th, you helped me by taking me to the grocery store after my car broke down.

_____

_____

_____

_____

_____

3. A brief expression of what the act or action meant to the sender (client) and or how it benefited him (her):

Example: I want to thank you for taking time out of your busy day to help me. Being able to get groceries meant that I had on hand what I needed to make my kids' lunches the next day.

_____

_____

_____

_____

_____

4. Closing salutation and signature:

_____

_____

_____

_____

_____

As clients become more comfortable with writing, they can change the structure of their notes. For example, a client may prefer to begin with, "I want to thank you for your act of kindness last week…." Encourage clients to keep their notes short and to the point. This will help clients to hone their words and better express themselves.

After completing the message, talk with the client to determine how the message will be delivered to the receiver. Keep in mind the cost of postage, access to e-mail, and any other barrier that may exist. Brainstorm about options as needed.

The primary purpose of the exercise is for the client to experience positive emotion around the appreciation for others. It is not necessary for the note to be sent for it to help the client experience the benefit of appreciating others on a more consistent basis. With this in mind, talk with the client about his (her) experience in writing the letter. Questions to ask include

- What was it like for you to write the note?
- What did you notice about how you felt?
- How is that different from the way you felt prior to writing the note?
- What is it like to know that you have just expressed something positive on paper to someone else?

- What could you do to on a more regular basis to let others know how much you appreciate them?
- How might that also benefit you?

A final aspect of this exercise is to encourage the expressions of gratitude to continue. Clients may choose to write a letter, an e-mail, or message a day, write several during a single sitting, and send them one at a time or all at once. After writing an expression of gratitude, suggest that the client take a moment to reflect on the positive emotions he (she) experienced.

References

Emmons, R. (2007). *Thanks: How the new science of gratitude can make you happier.* New York: Houghton Mifflin.
Peterson, C. (2006). *A primer in positive psychology.* New York: Oxford.

Gratitude "In Person"

Overview

In this book we offer various ideas for helping clients to express gratitude. This exercise involves more deliberate action on the part of clients by encouraging them to connect personally with the person or persons with whom they are wishing to express their gratitude. This exercise is influenced by the research, writing, and teaching of Martin Seligman. It also represents a variation of an exercise that has been found through a random-assignment, placebo-controlled study to increase levels of happiness at one month follow-up (Seligman, Steen, Park, & Peterson, 2005).

Suggestions for Use

This exercise is best for clients who are ready to express their gratitude in person. It involves having the client write out an expression of gratitude, rehearse it, and personally read it to the person to whom the client wishes to express gratitude. Because this exercise can involve intense emotion and a degree of readiness on the part of clients, it is recommended that it be discussed in detail before choosing it as an option. In addition, it may be helpful for clients to try other exercises in this book that focus on gratitude prior to this one. It should be noted that this exercise can also be used in conjunction with, "I Just Wanted You to Know" in Chapter 5. In such cases, clients can use the letter, e-mail, note, or artwork created in "I Just Wanted You to Know." When discussing this exercise with clients, be sure to go through each step in detail.

Exercise

This exercise involves the following steps.

1. Have the client write a letter of gratitude to a person from his (her) past. The letter should include something left unsaid that the client wishes to share. The letter and the process are meant to evoke positive emotion for the client. If the client has completed the exercise "I Just Wanted You to Know," the letter, e-mail, or note from that exercise can be used in its current or in a modified form.
2. After the letter has been completed, have the client read the letter aloud in private or in therapy. During the rereading process, have the client maintain eye contact with the person to whom the letter is being read. If the letter is being read in a therapy session, check in with the client to explore any emotions that arise. Remember that reading the letter should bring about far more positive than negative emotion. Have the client rehearse the letter as needed.
3. Have the client create a plan a visit to the person to whom he (she) wishes to express gratitude.
4. Have the client complete the visit and read the letter to that person.
5. After the letter has been read, the client should wait for the other person's response. Prior to this step, it is important to talk with the client about the importance of "sitting still" and letting the person to whom the letter has been read respond. The client should avoid expanding or elaborating on what has been written and just listen to and experience what the other person has to say.

6. Within a few hours (and as close in proximity as possible) of the expression of gratitude, have the client write the emotions that he (she) experienced.
7. If possible, talk with the client in person about his (her) experience in doing the exercise.

Reference

Seligman, M. E. P., Steen, T. A., Park, N., & Peterson, C. (2005). Positive psychology progress: Empirical validation of interventions. *American Psychologist, 60*(5), 410–421.

Contentment

Overview

We heard a story some time ago about a party the novelists Joseph Heller and Kurt Vonnegut attended in the Hamptons. It was held at a hedge fund trader's house in which the living room was bigger than most people's houses. Vonnegut was chiding Heller about the opulent wealth they saw before them. "Doesn't it make you envious that this fellow probably makes more in a day than you did from the life of your best-selling book, Joe?" Heller didn't bite. "Not a bit," he calmly replied, "because I have something that he doesn't have." "What could you possibly have that this fellow doesn't or couldn't buy at a moment's notice?" Vonnegut retorted. "I know the meaning of enough," Heller said.

And that is the essence and purpose of this exercise. To be content with having enough. Every year, the economy and businesses are expected to grow, to have more sales than last year. If they don't, it is seen as a sign of failure or trouble. Human evolution seems to have biased us to being unsatisfied and constantly seeking more, rarely resting in what we have. "The thought that life can be better is woven indelibly into our hearts and our brains," sings Paul Simon (1988). But this restlessness, this sense of things not being enough, or ourselves not being enough, does not lead to happiness or peace of mind.

This book was being written during an economic crisis. Bill had a strange reaction to seeing and reading all the bad news in the news media. He grew more and more content. He kept having the thought and sense: I have enough to eat; I feel pretty good; I have a place to live; I like my work and get meaning from it; I have people who love me and people I love. I have enough. Now this was a new experience for him. Consider that this book is his 31st. He is not one to rest in how things are. He was restless and always striving for the next ... whatever—book, level of impact with his work, relationship, success, and so on. This newly found contentment was unfamiliar and very calming. For the first time in years, he rested in how things were. He was content. A bit different from being happy. Merely at peace. It was nice.

In a group for people struggling with weight and body issues Bill led, the group was given the assignment to work on accepting themselves as they are at the moment. But one of the women in the group objected: "I'll never be able to accept myself at this weight," she avowed.

But the next week, when the group convened again, she quickly spoke up and said that she was on board with this task now. What had changed?, the group wanted to know. She said that she had been asked by a relative to find a photo he wanted of her mother. While looking through her photos, she had come across a photo of herself from five years back. She instantly had the thought, "If I weighed that, I could accept myself like they are asking me to do in that group." And just after that, she recalled how much she hated her weight and looks at that time. Now, looking back more objectively, she saw that she looked pretty good. She quickly realized that just as easily she could be looking back at herself someday five years in the future and thinking she looked pretty good at her current weight. Realizing that, she decided to work on self-acceptance.

Suggestions for Use

This exercise is primarily for clients who continue to feel a sense that they don't have enough, that happiness or contentment is just around the corner with the next accomplishment or achievement, or who are self-critical.

Exercise

Have the client complete the following series of activities.

- Have the client list all the things they have in their lives with which they are satisfied and those with which they are unsatisfied.

Satisfied	Unsatisfied

- Next, have the client run through the following series of scenarios to get some perspective.

Have the client look at that list, imagining that he (she) had just gotten the news that he (she) had an inoperable brain tumor (or other terminal illness) and had three months to live.

Have the client imagine he (she) is 90 years old and still dissatisfied, wanting to reach another level of success, recognition, or to have some other material possession.

Ask the client what it would take to be content or satisfied with themselves, his (her) level of success and achievement, or with the things he (she) currently has in life right now. What would it take to be content? Have the client live with that question for the next week or two.

Additional Resources

Bach, R. (1981). *Illusions: The adventures of a reluctant messiah.* New York: Laurel Books.

Nepo, M. (2000). *The book of awakening: Having the life you want by being present to the life you have.* Newburyport, MA: Conari Press.

Simon, P. (1988). Train in the distance. *On negotiations and love songs*, 1971–1986 [CD, remastered]. New York: Sterling Sound.

Mindfulness

Overview

People have the ability to merely observe their experience, including their suffering, their impulses, their feelings, their thoughts, and their responses, without have to react to or do anything about those experiences. Just noticing and staying with an experience may allow the person to dissolve or move through the experience, or it may give the person time to make different and better choices about how to respond. This ability is called "mindfulness" and what this exercise is about.

Derived from a Buddhist practice used for thousands of years, mindfulness has recently been secularized and applied to many aspects of life in Western cultures. It has also begun to be studied in the laboratory and connected to happiness. Richard Davidson (2010) has been using EEG and fMRI readings to investigate the effects of mindfulness meditation on people's stress levels and their happiness. Mindfulness as it is used in Western settings is essentially noticing without judgment what one is feeling or perceiving.

A 2003 study (Davidson et al., 2003) found that after two months of three hours per week practice of mindfulness meditation, brain scans showed that a group of highly stressed tech workers were activating the "happier" parts of their brains; they also reported feeling more engaged in their work, less stressed, and less anxious.

There have been other studies showing the benefits of mindfulness in decreasing anxiety and depression, which we know bring down happiness and well-being levels. In one study, subjects showed significant clinical improvements in symptoms of anxiety and panic following an eight-week mindfulness-based meditation stress reduction program in a study (Kabat-Zinn et al., 1992) of 22 medical outpatients who met DSM diagnosis for generalized anxiety or panic disorder with or without agoraphobia. Subjects improved in their self-rating scores of anxiety and depression (using the Beck anxiety and depression scales) and in interviewers' ratings (using the Hamilton anxiety and depression scales).

Three-year follow-up of 18 medical outpatients with anxiety disorders showed improvements in subjective and objective symptoms of anxiety and panic following an eight-week outpatient group intervention based on mindfulness-based stress reduction meditation showed maintenance of the gains obtained in the original study on depression and anxiety scales as well as on the number and severity of panic attacks. In a three year follow up after the conclusion of the experiment, most of the subjects continued with their meditation practice. (Miller, Fletcher, & Kabat-Zinn, 1995).

Suggestions for Use

Mindfulness is a bit different from savoring. In mindfulness, people are not appreciating the pleasurable experiences they are having, but more neutrally learning to just notice and be with those experiences. When they use mindfulness, people are witnessing without getting swept up in having to do anything about those experiences. They don't need to get rid of them or decide whether they are bad or good. They are just to notice them. Mindfulness can be used in relation to thoughts, sensations, feelings, states of mind, moods, the external world, and other people. It is a shifting of relationship from one of judgment and reaction to observing.

There was a story Bill read some years ago about a man who had tried everything to lose weight and keep it off, but to no avail. He knew everything about calories, nutrition, what he needed to eat, and how much he needed to be active to lose weight and keep it off, but he always seemed to succumb to temptation after losing weight and ended up right back where he started (or worse).

Finally, one day the man decided that no expert or diet plan could help him and that he would have to figure out the solution by himself. On a Saturday morning, he carefully prepared a healthy meal, ate it, and sat down to pay attention to what happened. Within an hour or so, he noticed that he had the urge to go eat something unhealthy. He resisted the urge and noticed that he began to be a little anxious. Still he sat and didn't get up to eat. The anxiety began to be more intense. It was all he could do to sit there and not get up to eat. He felt like he was going to crawl out of his skin, the anxiety was so overwhelming. Still he sat. The anxiety turned to fear. The fear turned to terror. He began to shake and sweat. But he was determined to get to the bottom of what was driving him to eat.

Those were the worst several hours of his life, he reported later. He was convinced that he would die from the sheer terror. He thought his heart might give out. But it did not and he didn't get up to eat. He sat there and felt it all. After several hours, it began to subside. Finally it dissipated entirely.

A little while later, he ate a healthy lunch and again sat to observe. In a short time, the urge to get up and eat again came upon him, followed by the anxiety and the fear, followed by the shaking and sweating terror session. But this time he was less terrified. He had already survived one of these torture sessions and was pretty sure he could survive again.

He had several other such sessions over the course of the weekend, each one a little less intense and a bit shorter. By the end of the weekend, the shaking and the sweating were down to 15 minutes of discomfort. And he had successfully avoided overeating. He used breaks to deal with it when he went back to work that week; and by the end of the week, he knew he had overcome overeating forever. He lost the weight and kept it off. He never did know what that unnamed terror was, but that wasn't relevant. He had unknowingly used mindfulness to resolve his weight issues.

Exercise

First, as a therapist, try this for yourself by following the steps outlined.

- Identify a place in your life when you are typically reactive in a way that doesn't serve you or others.
- Decide how you could use mindfulness (just noticing rather than doing anything) in that situation.
- The next time the situation or experience occurs, try using mindfulness. Just sit with it and notice for as long as you can and is appropriate.

Now, try using mindfulness with clients:

- When clients are experiencing something difficult, suggest they stop for a moment and just notice that experience. That is, to pay close attention to what they are experiencing without judging it or trying to get rid of it. Can they just let the experience be without deciding that it is good or bad or needing to do something about it?
- Suggest that clients practice mindfulness at home during significant moments. Remind clients to
- Pay full attention to whatever they can notice about the experience. This includes sensations, thoughts, judgments, feelings, physiological and neurological aspects of the experience, and perceptions.

Reference

Davidson, R. J. (2010). Empirical explorations of mindfulness: Conceptual and methodological conundrums. *Emotion, 10*(1), 8–11.

Davidson R. J., Kabat-Zinn, J., Schumacher, J., Rosenkranz, M., Muller, D., Santorelli, S. F., Urbanowski, F., Harrington, A., Bonus, Katherine, & Sheridan, J. F. (2003). Alterations in brain and immune function produced by mindfulness meditation. *Psychosomatic Medicine*, *65*(4), 564–570.

Kabat-Zinn, J., Massion, A., Kristeller, J., Peterson, L. G., Fletcher, K., Pbert, L., et al. (1992). Effectiveness of a meditation-based stress reduction program in the treatment of anxiety disorders. *American Journal of Psychiatry*, *149*, 936–943.

Miller, J., Fletcher, K., & Kabat-Zinn, J. (1995). Three-year follow-up and clinical implications of a mindfulness meditation-based stress reduction intervention in the treatment of anxiety disorders. *General Hospital Psychiatry*, *17*, 192–200.

Additional Resources

Brown, K., & Ryan, R. (2003). The benefits of being present: Mindfulness and its role in psychological wellbeing, *Journal of Personality and Social Psychology*, *84*, 822–848.

Carmody, J., & Baer, R. (2008). Relationships between mindfulness practice and levels of mindfulness, medical and psychological symptoms and well-being in a mindfulness-based stress reduction program, *Journal of Behavioral Medicine*, *31*, 23–33.

Chang, V., Palesh, O., Caldwell, R., Glasgow, N., Abramson, M., Luskin, F., et al. (2004). The effects of a mindfulness-based stress reduction program on stress, mindfulness self-efficacy, and positive states of mind. *Stress and Health: Journal of the International Society for the Investigation of Stress*, *20*, 141–147.

Davidson, R. J., & Lutz, A. (2008). Buddha's brain: Neuroplasticity and meditation. *IEEE Signal Processing*, *25*(1), 171–174.

Grepmair, L., Mitterlehner, F., Loew, T., Bachler, E., Rother, W., & Nickel, M. (2007). Promoting mindfulness in psychotherapists in training influences the treatment results of their patients: A randomized, double-blind, controlled study. *Psychotherapy and Psychosomatics*, *76*, 332–338.

Jacobs, B., & Nagel, L. (2003). The impact of a brief mindfulness-based stress reduction program on perceived quality of life. *International Journal of Self Help and Self Care*, *2*, 155–168.

Lutz, A., Greischar, L., Rawlings, N. B., Ricard, M., & Davidson, R. (2004). Long-term meditators self-induce high-amplitude synchrony during mental practice. *Proceedings of the National Academy of Sciences*, *101*, 16369–16373.

Ryff, C., Love, G., Urry, H., Muller, D., Rosenkranz, M., Friedman, E., Davidson, R., & Singer, B. (2006). Psychological well-being and ill-being: Do they have distinct or mirrored biological correlates? *Psychotherapy and Psychosomatics*, *75*, 85–95.

Mindfulness for Depression

Overview

In a previous section we detailed mindfulness. In the next few sections we show how mindfulness can be used to help in several different areas. The first one we take up, one that has a fair amount of research support, is the use of mindfulness to reduce depression and prevent relapses in depressive problems.

The purpose of this exercise is to help clients reduce their suffering by helping them notice sensations, feelings, thoughts, and experiences involved with their experience of depression, including any variations in the experience. We help them witness rather than get caught up in or carried away by the experience of depression. We ask them to become curious rather than reactive to depression.

Studies have been done using an amalgam of cognitive behavioral therapy and mindfulness called "mindfulness-based cognitive therapy," or MBCT. MBCT proved as effective as maintenance antidepressants in preventing a relapse and more effective in enhancing peoples' quality of life. One study (Kuyken et al., 2008) also showed MBCT to be as cost-effective as prescription drugs in helping people with a history of depression stay well in the longer term. Over the 15 months after the trial, 47% of the group following the MBCT course experienced a relapse compared with 60% of those continuing their normal treatment, including anti-depressant drugs. In addition, the group in the MBCT program reported a higher quality of life in terms of their overall enjoyment of daily living and physical well-being.

Suggestions for Use

Using mindfulness with depression might seem counterintuitive, but part of the suffering in depression is the meaning one gives to it and also what might be called "suffering about suffering." It's a bit like the fear of fear. When fear amplifies fear, it can get much worse. The same can occur when people are suffering from depression. They are already suffering, and their attempts to get rid of the suffering, or thinking that there is something fundamentally wrong with them (judging themselves harshly), or thinking they will never emerge from this dark phase of their life, or feeling guilty for being a burden on others, and so on, can add to their suffering.

Using mindfulness, we are having depression sufferers merely notice what their minds are telling them, what sensations they are having, what conclusions they are making, what neurological experiences they are having, and so on. This can remove one layer of suffering from the experience of depression.

Another way that mindfulness might be helpful in alleviating or helping prevent the recurrence of depression is to train people to notice variations in their depressive experience. We speak about "depression" as if it is the same experience for everyone, when it is probably different from person to person in its manifestation. In addition, there are, when one pays close attention, variations in the individual's ongoing experience of depression, and helping them attend to those variations can show them that change can occur and that there are moments of nondepression that occur in most depressive episodes.

Exercise

Discuss mindfulness with your depressed client. Say the following to your client:

- I want you to pay really close attention to the experience you have this next week with depression. In this approach, you will be just noticing, a bit like an anthropologist, studying the way depression manifests for you. Notice, without trying to interfere with or change anything, any sensations, thoughts, judgments, feelings, and physiological or neurological experiences related to depression.

- I am especially interested in any variations on the typical experience of depression you might notice.
- I am suggesting you take an attitude of curiosity in regard to depression.

After having the client complete this exercise, have him (her) report on the outcome.

Reference

Kuyken, W., Byford, S., Taylor, R. S., Watkins, E., Holden, E., White, K., Barrett, B., Byng, R., Evans, A., Mullan, E., & Teasdale, J. D. (2008). Mindfulness-based cognitive therapy to prevent relapse in recurrent depression. *Journal of Consulting and Clinical Psychology, 76*(6), 966–978.

Additional Resources

Barnhofer, T., Crane, C., Hargus, E., Amarasinghe, M., Winder, R., & Williams, J. M. G. (2009). Mindfulness-based cognitive therapy as a treatment for chronic depression: A preliminary study. *Behaviour Research and Therapy, 47*(5), 366–373.

Barnhofer, T., & Crane, C. (2008). Mindfulness-based cognitive therapy for depression and suicidality. In F. Didonna (Ed.), *Clinical handbook of mindfulness.* New York: Springer.

Bondolfi, G., Jermann, F., Der Linden, M. V., Gex-Fabry, M., Bizzini, L., Rouget, B. W., Myers-Arrazola, L., Gonzalez, C., Segal, Z, Aubry, J. M., & Bertschy, G. (2010). Depression relapse prophylaxis with mindfulness-based cognitive therapy: Replication and extension in the Swiss health care system. *Journal of Affective Disorders, 122*(3), 224–231.

Teasdale, J. D., Moore, R. G., Hayhurst, H., Pope, M., Williams, S., & Segal, Z. V. (2002). Metacognitive awareness and prevention of relapse in depression: Empirical evidence. *Journal of Consulting and Clinical Psychology, 70*(2), 275–287.

Teasdale, J. D., Segal, Z. V., Williams, J. M. G., Ridgeway, V. A., Soulsby, J. M., & Lau, M.A. (2000). Prevention of relapse/recurrence in major depression by mindfulness-based cognitive therapy. *Journal of Consulting and Clinical Psychology, 68*(4), 615–623.

Teasdale, J. D., Segal, Z. V., Williams, J. M. G., Ridgeway, V., Lau, M., & Soulsby, J. (2000). Reducing risk of recurrence of major depression using mindfulness-based cognitive therapy. *Journal of Consulting and Clinical Psychology, 68*, 615–623.

Williams, M., Teasdale, J., Segal, Z., & Kabat-Zinn, J. (2007). *The mindful way through depression: Freeing yourself from chronic unhappiness.* New York: Guilford.

Mindfulness in Relationships: Noticing without Judging

Overview

Mindfulness can also be helpful in relationships. Much of the time in ongoing relationships, we begin to get used to and take for granted, others with whom we relate regularly. We stop noticing things about them.

When we first meet someone in a romantic relationship, most of us are fascinated and curious. We notice the stray hair, the facial expression, the sigh, the new piece of clothing. We hang on to their every word. We are paying close attention to our loved one. But as time goes on, that newness begins to fade and we have a sense that we already know the person, the kinds of things they will say, how they will dress and act, and we stop attending so closely. This is natural and built into our neurology and our brains.

But it can also lead to the illusion that the other person is staying the same, when actually they might be changing and we don't notice. In addition, we are less interested, and that may translate into less emotional intensity and connection. Our partners, friends, family members, and co-workers are probably not getting the same affectionate or interested "vibe" from us.

One way to make relationships better then is to become more mindful of them. This means paying attention in a nonjudgmental way. The purpose of this exercise is to help clients increase their mindfulness in relationships.

Suggestions for Use

This exercise can be given to one or both people in any kind of relationship—romantic/sexual, family, friend, or work. The objective is a renewal of the relationship and a renewed appreciation of the other person in the relationship. You could think of it as a "wake-up call," as we are often sleep-walking through our relationships after being in them for some time.

Exercise

Discuss mindfulness in relationships with your client. Tell him (her) the following:

• After being in any relationship for some time, we often stop noticing things about the other person in such an intense way. It's just the way our brains work. We start to take for granted things we see regularly. But this can diminish our relationships. In reality, both you and the other person are changing a little much of the time. And paying attention to those changes can bring about a newfound appreciation and renewal of your relationships.

• I want you to pay really close attention to the other person this next week. Just notice, a bit like an anthropologist, the way the other person speaks and moves. Notice what they are wearing and the expression on their face. Notice the tone in their voice. Notice their habits and the little quirks that make them unique. As much as you can, notice without judging or reacting. It will be as if you are an impartial, outside observer who is just curious about this being in front of you.

• You might have to remind yourself to pay attention. If you have spent a fair amount of time around the person, you will have a tendency to "go unconscious," forgetting to notice and attend.

• Also, do your best not to react or take things they say or do personally. As much as possible, just observe and be curious, as if you don't know the person or have a stake in what they say or do.

• I look forward to your report next time we meet. I'll be curious about what you observed, what your experience with this exercise is, and how it might change your relationship.

Resource

Carson, J., Carson, K., Gil, K., & Baucom, D. (2004). Mindfulness-based relationship enhancement. *Behavior Therapy*, *35*, 471–494.

Mindfulness in Relationships: Noticing Exceptions

Overview

Another way to use mindfulness in relationships is to encourage people to appreciate ongoing differences in their partners, husbands, or wives. We usually begin to see our partners as being about the same all the time. We generalize and stop noticing when little or big changes happen.

Couples often fall into ruts of relating and perceiving. And they fall into patterns of disappointment and judgment. "You are always late." "All you are interested in is sex." "You care about the kids more than you care about me." "There you go, always taking her side." Mindfulness can be a way to shift these disappointments and judgments and thereby enhance the appreciation in the relationship. This exercise is about this kind of mindfulness. Specifically, Ellen Langer and Leslie Coates Burpee (Burpee & Langer, 2005) found that couples' relationships are more rewarding when partners use mindfulness to notice variations in their partners rather than generalizing ("You are always distracted." or "You are never spontaneous.").

Suggestions for Use

This exercise can be helpful when couples have persistent complaints about one another as well as when one or both partners are bored or say they don't feel a sense of love any longer. The objective is a renewal of the relationship and to use mindfulness to challenge generalizations either partner has made about the other.

Exercise

Discuss mindfulness in relationships with your client. Tell them the following:

- Rarely is a person one way all the time. There are usually exceptions to any rule.
- Your task for the next while is to be like an investigator in your relationship, discovering times when the person does something a little (or a lot) out of their usual patterns. You will have to pay close attention to discover these variations; sometimes they may be subtle and hard to notice.
- You might have to remind yourself to pay attention. If you have spent a fair amount of time around the person, you will have a tendency to "go unconscious," forgetting to notice and attend.
- I want you to especially notice exceptions to anything your partner usually does that has bugged you. For example, if they are usually late, notice when they show up on time. If they usually forget to hang up the towel, notice the one time they do hang it up, and so on.
- I look forward to your report next time we meet. I'll be curious about what you observed and what your experience with this exercise is and how it might change your relationship.

Reference

Burpee, L., & Langer, E. (2005). Mindfulness and marital satisfaction. *Journal of Adult Development*, *12*, 43–51.

In the Living Years

Overview

There is a ritual that is commonplace at memorial services, particularly in North America—the eulogy. The idea of the eulogy is a wonderful one. It's an opportunity for loved ones and admirers to express their love, appreciation, and gratitude to the person who has passed on. But there is, of course, a downside. The person who the eulogy is for is no longer alive. The purpose of this exercise is to create an opportunity for a person who is admired to hear all the wonderful things that would be said about him (her) while he (she) is in the living years. This process allows people to openly convey their appreciation to a loved one and for the loved one to experience that gratitude in the present.

Suggestions for Use

This exercise is for clients who wish to express their appreciation to others. To set up this exercise, it can be helpful to have clients think of and write the things they would say about a particular person after he (she) passed away. A difference between this exercise and an everyday expression of gratitude is that this exercise is best done with a group of people present. So clients should be encouraged to include others in this exercise, with each person having an opportunity to express themselves.

Exercise

Have the client identify a person with whom he (she) would like to express gratitude. Next, suggest that the client choose other persons who might also appreciate the opportunity to do the same. Arrange for all persons involved to be present, but do not tell the person who will be receiving the gratitude about the situation. This will make the expression more spontaneous. Discuss the purpose of a "living eulogy" with those you have invited (but not the recipient). Then follow the steps below.

1. Name the person who will be receiving the gratitude:

   _____

   _____

   _____

2. Prepare a brief statement of not more than three minutes when said verbally, expressing your gratitude, appreciation, or acknowledgment of the person. Try to remain focused in your comments, making sure to address the things you want the person most to hear. Write your statement in the space below.

   _____

   _____

   _____

   _____

   _____

   _____

_____

_____

_____

_____

_____

_____

_____

_____

_____

_____

_____

_____

_____

_____

_____

_____

_____

_____

_____

_____

3. Ask others who have been invited to also create brief statements of not more than three minutes in length when said verbally.
4. At the arranged time, gather together and tell the recipient that you have come together as a group to celebrate his (her) life in the living years. Ask that the recipient wait until the process is complete and everyone has spoken before speaking.
5. Ask each person to go around in a circle and present his (her) prepared statement.
6. Invite the person who is the recipient of the living eulogy to share his (her) thoughts and feelings.
7. Celebrate with food and drink!

Suggestion: You or your client might want to listen to the song "The Living Years," by Mike & The Mechanics for inspiration for and perspective on this task.

Additional Resource

Albom, M. (1997). *Tuesdays with Morrie: An old man, a young man, and life's greatest lesson.* New York: Doubleday.

Identifying Mentors and Blessors

Overview

Often we have gotten to the place we have reached in life not only due to our parents and families, but also by being influenced, inspired, and encouraged by mentors and people who have believed in and blessed us with their interest and urging to go in a certain direction and to trust and believe in our capabilities.

Sometimes we don't even have to meet these people to be positively influenced by them. Bill was inspired from afar by Jay Haley, a family therapist who, like Bill, had only a master's degree in a field dominated by Ph.D.s, and who also wrote articles and books and taught workshops that fundamentally influenced and changed the field of therapy. Because Bill had that calling, he had a sense of the possibility that he could do the same, opened by following Haley's work. They did not meet until many years later, but Haley was an influential role model for Bill, and the influence was there nonetheless.

Sometimes people appear at just the right moments in our lives and say something significant to us that changes our thinking or the course of our lives in a new and helpful direction. We can think of those people as secular angels in our lives. Sometimes these people have validated us or some way we think or some way we are. Sometimes we get important permission from these people. Sometimes they bless us. The purpose of this exercise is designed to highlight the appreciation we have for those mentors, models, angels, and other positive influencers in our clients' lives.

Suggestions for Use

The idea here is to help people appreciate those people who were (or are) positive influences or inspirations for them. We sometimes think we arrived at any successes or better places in our lives due solely to our own efforts, and this is a reminder that it usually takes a village (or at least one other person) to make a successful life or transition to a new place in life.

Exercise

Investigate mentors, positive and inspiring role models, and angels in your clients' lives. Then help them recognize and appreciate those people.

- Who has taken a special interest in you and encouraged you?

    _____

    _____

- Who believes or believed in you?

    _____

    _____

- Who has been or is your mentor?

    _____

    _____

- Who have been your inspirational models?

    _____

    _____

- Who has blessed you?

  _____

  _____

- Who has been your angel?

  _____

  _____

- What did that person or those people contribute to your life?

  _____

  _____

- How did they bless you?

  _____

  _____

- How did they show you a direction for your life?

  _____

  _____

- What permission did they give you?

  _____

  _____

- What validation did they provide?

  _____

  _____

- What encouragement did they give you?

  _____

  _____

- What inspiration did they provide?

  _____

  _____

Additional Resource

Johnson, W., & Ridley, C. (2004). *The elements of mentoring.* New York: Palgrave Macmillan.

Visiting Graceland

Overview

In several religious and spiritual traditions, there is a notion of grace or something akin to grace. Grace is unearned blessings of the good things in one's life. Being born in a certain country to certain parents and therefore having enough nutrition and prenatal care in the womb and in childhood could be seen as an unearned blessing. Being born with certain talents or abilities. Receiving unexpected and unearned kindnesses from people in the course or life could qualify as grace as well.

Being cognizant of and expressing appreciation for grace could increase one's life satisfaction and happiness. Philosopher Epictetus wrote: "He is a wise man who does not grieve for the things which he has not, but rejoices for those which he has." But some of those things we have clearly come from our own efforts. Grace covers the things that came without our efforts and unbidden. This exercise is about helping clients experience and appreciate grace in their lives.

Suggestions for Use

The idea here is to help people become aware of and appreciate those things they did nothing to create. The hope is that this appreciation will increase their sense of well-being and happiness.

Exercise

For this exercise, have the client answer the following questions.

- Make a list of good things in your life that you had nothing to do with creating or putting there.

_____

_____

_____

_____

_____

- What healthy, nice life circumstances and conditions were you born into that many people in the world don't or didn't have?

_____

_____

- What luxuries do we in the modern world take for granted that previous generations did not have?

_____

_____

- Take some time each week and ponder these unearned benefits in your life.

    _____

    _____

- Write them on paper or discuss them if that helps you appreciate them more.

    _____

    _____

- When you have the odd free moment here and there, cast your mind to your blessings and the grace in your life. You can train your attention toward gratitude for unearned good things (or grace) in your life.

    _____

    _____

- Notice the cumulative effect of this practice after one month. Decide if you want to keep it going.

Additional Resources

Emmons, R. (2007). *Thanks: How the new science of gratitude can make you happier.* New York: Houghton Mifflin.

Emmons, R. A., & McCullough, M. E. (2003). Counting blessings versus burdens: An experimental investigation of gratitude and subjective well-being in daily life. *Journal of Personality and Social Psychology, 84*(2), 377–389.

6

Talk Positively

This chapter helps both clients and therapists shift from a more negative focus to a more positive one. In part, this is done with language. People live in a sea of language, and positively oriented talk influences thinking and feeling.

Because therapy has traditionally been biased toward the problematic in discussions in sessions, it takes some deliberate effort to shift the conversation in a new direction.

We heard a story about a man walking down the street and coming upon the scene of a house ablaze. The firefighters were battling the blaze. The man walked up to the fire chief and asked, "That looks pretty bad. Do you think you can save it?" The fire chief thought for a minute and then said, "Yes, if there's a shift in the wind." In this chapter, we show you how to use language to be that "shift in the wind."

Start with a Smile

Overview

It has been estimated that there are over 20,000 moments in a given day to positively influence another's life. Many times a seemingly small, insignificant gesture can change the course of a person's day. There is more good news. The person who extends a smile, expresses a kind or encouraging word, or comes to another's aid also benefits. This is because acknowledgment and gratitude are gifts that boost levels of happiness for all involved. The purpose of this exercise is to help clients to more consciously express kindness, gratitude, and happiness in the form of small gestures.

There is some evidence that smiling creates a better mood within people (Adelmann & Zajonc, 1989; McIntosh, 1996; Strack, Martin, & Stepper, 1988). This is called the "facial feedback hypothesis." One feels one's mouth smile and the brain decides that one must be happy or amused, thus creating more positive affect.

Suggestions for Use

This exercise is for all clients. The only requirement of the client is a willingness to make other people's lives a little better, if even for a moment. For this exercise, suggest that clients experiment with small gestures such as smiles, saying "thank you," opening doors for others, or asking "How are you today?" There will be clients who will say, "I already do that" or "What difference will that really make?" Encourage such clients to continue with the gestures they already do in the course of a day and then to increase their expressions by 20%. For example, instead of smiling only at people in the office, have the client smile at five people on the street during the day. In terms of the difference it might make in other's lives, encourage clients to "experiment" and see. It might also be helpful to ask clients what it is like for them when someone smiles at them. Finally, some clients might better understand by watching the movie, *Pay it Forward* (2000), in which a young boy does something nice for three people, who each do the same for three others, and so on. Kindness is spread through selfless acts.

Exercise

For this exercise, have the client complete the following steps.

1. Identify as many of the "common" things you do during the course of your day that either make others happy or let others know you are thinking of them. No matter how small the act, include it in your list. Examples might be making eye contact, smiles, kisses, saying "hello," waving goodbye, opening doors for others, etc.

_____   _____

_____   _____

_____   _____

_____   _____

_____   _____

2. Estimate the number of times during the course of a day that you extend a gesture of kindness.

_____

3. For the next day, increase the level that you estimated for Step 2 by 20%.
4. At the end of your day, write about what it was like for you to increase your expression of kindness.

_____

_____

_____

_____

_____

_____

5. Next, think of a few specific things that you might do to extend yourself to others just a little more. Keep the ideas small but potentially meaningful. Make a list of those things in the space below.

_____   _____

_____   _____

_____   _____

_____   _____

_____   _____

6. Select two or three things from your list and try them out over the next week.

7. In the space below, write about how your experience of trying those new expressions worked. What specifically was it like for you?

_____

_____

_____

_____

_____

_____

8. Make a plan to keep it up!

References

Adelmann, P. K., & Zajonc, R. B. (1989). Facial efference and the experience of emotion. *Annual Review of Psychology, 40*, 249–280.

McIntosh, D. N. (1996). Facial feedback hypotheses: Evidence, implications, and directions. *Motivation and Emotion, 20*(2), 121–147.

Strack, F., Martin, L., & Stepper, S. (1988). Inhibiting and facilitating conditions of the human smile: A nonobtrusive test of the facial feedback hypothesis. *Journal of Personality and Social Psychology, 54*, 768–777.

Backward Positive Talk

Overview

Many clients arrive in a negative mood due to the problems and suffering they are experiencing. They may have had other experiences with therapy that have left them cynical and suspicious. Or perhaps they have a tendency to be cranky, pessimistic, and negative. For these clients, we often use a backward way of eliciting a type of positive report or talk. We ask them why their problems aren't worse. We are not trying to be provocative with this line of inquiry, but rather to determine, in a backward way, some resources and abilities they have that perhaps they haven't recognized. That is the purpose of this exercise.

Bill had a client come to see him who was struggling with severe obesity. He said he was out of control. By coincidence, Bill had just come from the grocery store and while standing in the checkout line he had glanced at the cover headline and photo on one of those tabloid newspapers so common these days. The headline read: "1,200-pound man eats 30 T-bone steaks a day!" It had a photo of the alleged 1,200-pound man *sans* shirt. Bill mentioned this to his new client. "You say you are out of control, but how come you don't weigh 1,200 pounds?" "Oh, I would never let myself go like that," the client replied. "When I hit 225, I vowed I wouldn't get a pound heavier and started cutting back on my eating. I can't afford to buy new clothes and I still have some pride left. That's why I am here. I don't ever want to weigh that much." There followed some discussion of how he managed to keep from gaining more weight, and he soon realized that he wasn't entirely out of control. Resources like his sense of pride (and shame), his ability to modify his eating habits, and his unwillingness to spend more money on clothes became helpful as the work proceeded.

When clients arrive at our offices complaining of depression that keeps them unable to get out of bed in the morning, we might inquire about how they got themselves to the appointment, and we hear about friends or family members who helped them or their commitment to keeping their appointments because they gave their word, or how their desire to get out of this depression was stronger than the depression at the moment of getting out of bed. All of these can be the seeds or platforms for further changes.

Suggestions for Use

This exercise, for therapists, works with most clients but is most suited for the more negative, skeptical, cynical, or "resistant" client. We sometimes think of this as clients who have their keys upside down. If you try to ask them about resources, strengths, solutions, or things that have gone well, you get no response or a negative, upset response. It's as if you tried unlocking a door and the key didn't fit the way you first tried to insert it. Try upending the key and it works (provided it is the right key, of course).

Exercise

In the most respectful and nonprovocative way you can, ask clients why their problems aren't worse. Listen for solutions, strengths, and resources. Those resources may be interpersonal or contextual and do not always have to reflect the client's own efforts. Here are some sample questions. Create your own based on these models and personalized to your client's circumstances and sensibilities.

- Why isn't the problem worse? I have had clients who couldn't get out of bed and, as difficult as it is for you, most days you do manage to get yourself up. How do you do that? How do you explain that your depression hasn't kept you bedridden?

_____

_____

_____

- Wow! You have struggled with suicide since you were nine. You have made it to 29 so far. How do you explain that suicide hasn't claimed you yet?

_____

_____

_____

- Some people dealing with gambling problems have lost their houses and their cars. You haven't. What do you think has kept you from going all the way down that far?

_____

_____

_____

Additional Resources

Bertolino, B., & O'Hanlon, B. (2001). *Collaborative, competency-based counseling and therapy*. Needham Heights, MA: Allyn & Bacon.
O'Hanlon, B., & Beadle, S. (1998). *A guide to possibility land*. New York: W. W. Norton.

Ac-cen-tchu-ate the Positive

Overview

An old song gave us the title for this exercise. Accentuate the positive, however, must not be seen as mere positive thinking. It is a leaning on the side of what works rather than focusing on what is wrong. It is noticing and highlighting strengths rather than focusing on deficits. That is the main point of this exercise.

Even the term "Pollyanna," used as a pejorative for people who only see the bright side (Ehrenreich, 2010) of things to the point of denial of any negative or bad thing, is misused. If one reads the book from which that term springs (Porter, 2010), one will find that Pollyanna is a little girl in bad circumstances who shifts almost everyone around her by treating them with trust and seeing the best in them. In response, those people rise to their better selves and feel sympathy and connection with this kind and loving little girl. In response to that, her circumstances improve.

We prefer the term "possibility," which includes a recognition of the problems and negatives while leaning toward the possibility that change can occur and, like young Pollyanna, that bringing out the best in people—their strengths, their best motives, their capabilities, their own intrinsic knowledge and solutions—can be an effective way to create positive change. In life and in therapy.

Suggestions for Use

In this method, we are paying close attention to reports and hints about what works in the client's life while recognizing what doesn't work. We tend to talk about "marbling" in inquiries about what works with acknowledgments of problems, setbacks, and suffering. We attend to the problem side of things in therapy while staying vigilant in noticing and highlighting what is going well or previous solutions.

In this exercise, which is for therapists, we suggest you train yourself to go, like a heat-seeking missile, toward any reports or hints of things that are working. For example, if the client says, "Right after my last appointment, things were great for a few days, but then everything went to hell," we would tend to first ask about what happened during those first few days. All too often, we therapists get hooked by reports of trouble and suffering and never get back to what went well and whether that could help prevent or recover from such troubles.

Exercise

Your mission, should you accept it, is to turn yourself into a solution-noticing machine. Your radar should be tuned to listen for what is working, for solutions, for strengths, and for exceptions to the usual problems and problematic ways of coping.

It can be a difficult transition to make if you have a problem- or pathology-oriented background or training as a therapist, so we'll take it in baby steps (and yes, we hope you just thought about the movie *What About Bob?* and had a good chuckle).

- For one week, listen for any reports of what went well or better from the client. When you hear anything that sounds remotely like a report of one of those things, when the moment is right, ask more details about what happened and how the client experienced it.
- For the second week, tune yourself to listen for any evidence or reports of client strengths (from the client or someone else). Again, in a respectful way, become curious about those strengths. Be careful of pushing your view on the client or becoming a cheerleader—this can sometimes get a bad counter-reaction. Just be curious and let the client tell you about these things.

- For the third week, notice when the client had coped in a better way than usual. This doesn't mean that the client has solved or avoided the problem, but rather that he (she) used a different way of coping that wasn't as problematic or self-harming. Again, explore this in detail with the client.

References

Ehrenreich, B. (2010). *Bright-sided: How positive thinking is undermining America.* New York: Picador.
O'Hanlon, B., & Beadle, S. (1998). *A guide to possibility land.* New York: W. W. Norton.
Porter, E. (1913/2010). *Pollyanna.* Seattle, WA: Amazon/Nabu Press.

Repeat After Me

Overview

Researcher Emoto (2004, 2007) found that language and different forms of vibration affect the molecular composition of water crystals. In his studies, he exposed cylinders of water to harsh, loud sounds and then to soft, soothing sounds. He then used a high-power microscope to photograph the crystals under both conditions. Emoto found that water crystals exposed to the "negative energy" of harsh, loud sounds exhibited fragmentation and what appeared to be disease-like qualities. In contrast, the water that had been exposed to the "positive energy" of soft, soothing sounds often revealed crystals that appeared to be growing and expanding. While controversial, whether or not these findings are replicated, the sentiment seems sound and in line with other findings in Positive Psychology. The purpose of this exercise is to encourage the use of positive language and vibration to increase positive states and subsequent well-being.

Suggestions for Use

This exercise can be used with all clients. It may be particularly useful with clients whose orientation is toward using more pessimistic or negative language. The idea is to help clients make subtle shifts to more positive language, noting the difference in how they feel within their bodies. From there we want to encourage clients to start to change their everyday statements about themselves, others, and the world around them.

Exercise

For this exercise, have the client complete the following steps.

1. Slowly repeat the following words aloud:

    Sad, Helpless, Inconvenienced, Bored, Defeated, Tired, Lonely, Doubtful, Uninterested

2. Next, read aloud the following statement:

    Life is so hard. Nothing seems to go my way. There is no one to turn to or count on. It feels like I've been forgotten. Times are tough. Nothing helps. Things will not get better. In fact, they will probably get worse. There is no hope.

3. What did you notice about how you felt from reading the preceding words (Step 1) and statement (Step 2)? What were your internal sensations? What did you think? Write your reactions in the space below.

    _____

    _____

    _____

    _____

4. Now let's change things up. Slowly repeat the following words aloud:

    Exciting, Fun, Laughter, Joy, Anticipation, Attractive, Possibility, Aliveness, Peace, Love

5. Next, read aloud the following statement:

   When I think about the future, I become excited. I'm energized. There is so much I can accomplish. Life is wonderful, and there are so many possibilities in the world.

6. What did you notice about how you felt from reading the preceding words (Step 4) and statement (Step 5)? What were your internal sensations? What did you think? Write your reactions in the space below.

   _____

   _____

   _____

   _____

7. What do you notice when you compare your experiences in Step 3 with those in Step 6? What was different?
8. Over the next week, consider how you can make changes to the statements you make about yourself, others, and the world around you. Note any differences in how you feel when you change statements that might otherwise be negative to positive ones.

References

Emoto, M. (2004). *The hidden messages in water.* Hillsboro, OR: Beyond Words Publishing.
Emoto, M. (2007). *The healing power of water.* Carlsbad, CA: Hay House.

Watching Our Words

Overview

Language can influence what we think, how we feel emotionally, and what we experience inside our bodies. Unfortunately, the field of mental health has become plagued with language that is based on pathology and problems. The purpose of this exercise is to encourage language that is empowering and emphasizes solutions versus problems.

Suggestions for Use

This exercise can be used with all clients. Our aim is to help clients identify the core language they use to refer to themselves, others, and the world around them. Because some words become part of our everyday vocabulary and we use them automatically, it's a good idea to begin by focusing on those words most common to clients. From there we can help them change statements. For an even greater impact, this exercise can be paired with "Repeat After Me" in Chapter 6.

Exercise

For this exercise, please complete the following steps.

1. Review the words in the two columns listed. Notice the differences between the sets of words.

Fix	→	Empower
Weakness	→	Strength
Limitation	→	Possibility
Pathology	→	Health
Problem	→	Solution
Insist	→	Invite
Closed	→	Open
Shrink	→	Expand
Defense	→	Access
Expert	→	Partner
Control	→	Nurture
Backward	→	Forward
Manipulate	→	Collaborate
Fear	→	Hope
Cure	→	Growth
Stuck	→	Change
Missing	→	Latent
Resist	→	Utilize
Past	→	Future
Hierarchical	→	Horizontal
Diagnose	→	Appreciate
Treat	→	Facilitate
End	→	Beginning
Judge	→	Respect
Never	→	Not yet
Limit	→	Expand
Defect	→	Asset
Rule	→	Exception

What stood out for you in terms of differences between the words? What implications might there be for you in using words in one column versus the other column?

When you are ready, move on to the next part of the activity.

2. In the left column are examples of words and phrases we commonly use without much deliberate thought. The problem with these words and phrases is that they carry a negative connotation for most people. The first few words and phrases in the left column are accompanied by alternative, more hopeful words, phrases, or descriptions in the right column. Note the differences between the two columns. In the last few spaces in the right column, think of words or phrases you can use to respond to those in the left column.

Negative/Problem-Focused	Positive/Strengths-Focused
Reactive	Is very sensitive to surroundings and changes
Attention deficit	Short attention span sometimes
Moody	Experiences things deeply
Annoying	Stands out
Isolates	Is introspective
Troublemaker	_____
Disruptive	_____
Manipulative	_____

What did you learn by changing the language between the two columns? What effect might it have if you were to make changes to your language in your everyday life? Over the next week, practice changing your language and report back on how it went for you.

3. For this final step, write any negative statements you catch yourself using or that you hear from others. Then revise those statements to reflect a new, more optimistic outlook. Also write the new statements you develop.

Negative Statement: _____

Revision: _____

Negative Statement: _____

Revision: _____

Negative Statement: _____

Revision: _____

Negative Statement: _____

Revision: _____

Negative Statement: _____

Revision: _____

Additional Resources

Bertolino, B. (2010). *Strengths-based engagement and practice: Creating effective helping relationships.* Boston, MA: Allyn & Bacon.

Bertolino, B., Kiener, M. S., & Patterson, R. (2009). *The therapist's notebook for strengths and solution-based therapies: Homework, handouts, and activities.* New York: Routledge/Taylor & Francis.

Bertolino, B., & Schultheis, G. (2002). *The therapist's notebook for families: Solution-oriented exercises for working with parents, children, and adolescents.* New York: The Haworth Press.

Acknowledgments versus Praise

Overview

Psychologist Ray Levy (Levy, O'Hanlon, & Goode, 2002) specializes in working with challenging children, typically diagnosed as ADHD or oppositional defiant. He has a simple method that can be very helpful in dealing with these and other children. It could also be used with adults as a way to shift the conversation from negatives to positives, which is the purpose of this exercise.

Levy holds that giving children praise for normal, expected behavior sets the parents and kids up for escalating misbehavior. That expectation should be built into daily life. For example, if a child sits quietly at the dinner table and doesn't get up and walk around or kick one of his siblings under the table, parents, teachers, or caregivers should not praise the child for not acting up.

But because the child had been misbehaving, it is important to acknowledge that shift. It is all too easy not to notice the "normal" or the lack of bad behavior. So Levy suggests just mentioning the everyday behavior to the child. "I noticed you sat quietly at dinner, Josh."

This rather simple idea and distinction can have profound effects. The child is "reinforced" by the attention he has received for normal, expected behavior but because it hasn't come in the form of praise, it gives the message that this is nothing special, but expected. No reward is given for this normal expected behavior. And the typical interaction parents have been having with such children (full of conflicts and negatives) is not happening at these moments of acknowledgment.

Suggestions for Use

This method can be used by parents, caregivers, or therapists.

To use acknowledgments, it is important to drop value judgments and value-laden words from the acknowledgment statements. Therefore, "You finished your chores on time. That was very good, Timmy," wouldn't be appropriate. Say simply, "You finished your chores on time," or "I noticed you finished your chores on time."

And avoid the temptation for scolding for previously bad behavior along with the acknowledgments. And skip the moral lesson as well. No, "See how easy it was to get your chores done on time and how well we get along when you do what you are supposed to do. Now, why couldn't you have done that yesterday?"

The net effect should be a decrease in negative talk and interactions between parents and children and an increase in positives (or at least neutrals).

Now, as you and the parents may discover, this is easier said than done and may take some practice.

Exercise

For this exercise, have the clients follow the instructions described below.

This is a method called acknowledgments. With this method, you are to avoid giving your child praise for normal, expected behavior. You are only to notice and comment on his behavior when he does something that is a positive, everyday cooperative or responsible behavior. You may have to really pay attention to notice these things, as you may have been vigilantly watching for bad behavior and may miss these everyday actions.

- Catch your child doing something right and not misbehaving.
- If this lack of bad behavior or good behavior is something that you expect most well-behaved and responsible children to do in your family or everyday life, just make a brief comment describing the behavior to the child.
  - For example, "I noticed you brushed your teeth." Or "You hung up your coat."
  - Keep your tone as neutral as possible. No sarcasm or praise or astonishment.

- Avoid the temptation to scold for past behavior.
- Avoid the temptation to add a moral lesson.
- Avoid value-laden words ("good," "bad," etc.).
- Notice the effect on your child after you master this and use it for some time. Do you notice anything different?

Reference

Levy, R., O'Hanlon, B., with Goode, T. (2002). *Try and make me: Simple strategies to turn off the tantrums and create cooperation.* New York: Signet.

Praise for Actions Not Qualities

Overview

A while ago, an experiment was done that had a surprising result. Psychologist and educational researcher Carol Dweck and colleagues wanted to find out whether the kind of praise one gave children made a positive or negative difference in their subsequent performance. Dweck and colleagues (Cimpian, Arce, Markman, & Dweck, 2007) gave children a fairly simple puzzle and told half the kids a comment that told them they were **smart** and the other half that **they must have worked hard to solve the puzzles**. Then they offered all of them a choice of simple or challenging puzzles. Ninety percent of the kids who were praised for effort chose the difficult puzzles; a majority of the kids who were praised for intelligence chose the easier ones. Next all the kids were given some more difficult puzzles. Then they were all given some puzzles that were about as easy as the initial ones. The "work hard" kids did 30% better than they had in the initial scores, while the "intelligence" kids' scores declined by 20%.

Their explanation, after observing and talking to the children, was that the "smart" kids were concerned about doing poorly on subsequent tasks and therefore avoided more challenging ones. They didn't want to lose their reputation for being smart. Therefore, they didn't challenge themselves and develop their puzzle-solving abilities (Dweck, 2007).

In contrast, those kids who were told that they must have worked hard attributed their performance to their efforts, so they worked harder and chose the harder puzzles when they had a choice. Therefore, they learned more by the end of the experiment.

Dweck went on to use these findings and follow children for some years. She taught children that the brain is like a muscle and that if they weren't doing well in some subjects, they could deliberately practice and challenge themselves and substantially improve their skills and grades in those areas. The children who came to believe this mind-set were able to make significant improvements in the years following this instruction (Dweck, 2007).

This mind-set fits well with modern understandings of brain functioning (Doidge, 2007). The brain appears to be plastic during the entire course of life—within some limits, of course. Repetitive and deliberate practice can change the speed and capabilities of the brain and neurology.

Suggestions for Use

Understanding this research shows us that as therapists, perhaps we should be careful about giving compliments or praise for our clients' qualities, but should probably notice things they have done well and attribute that performance to their efforts and actions instead.

In philosophy, this is called "personal agency," reflecting the idea that someone is an active agent in the situation rather than a passive recipient.

Exercise

For this exercise, as a therapist, focus on the following areas:

- Catch your client doing something well.
- Attribute, through statements or questions, that good performance to their efforts.
- You might ask: *How did you do that? Or How did you get that to happen?*
- Or use a comment or reflection that indicates that you notice or assume that they have made an effort to make something good happen.
- Some sample statements: *That must have taken some real restraint.* Or, *You got him to behave; it sounds like that took some doing.*

References

Cimpian, A., Arce, H. M. C., Markman, E. M., & Dweck, C. S. (2007). Subtle linguistic clues affect children's motivation. *Psychological Science, 18*(4), 314–316.

Doidge, N. (2007). *The brain that changes itself.* New York: Penguin.

Dweck, C. (2007). *Mindset: The new psychology of success.* New York: Ballantine.

Active Constructive Responding (ACR)

Overview

How people respond to each other is crucial to the quality of their relationships. In some cases the effects can be dramatic. Researcher Shelly Gable (Gable & Poore, 2008; Gable, Reis, Impett, & Asher, 2004) has indicated that how couples discuss good events is more predictive of strong relationships than how they fight. The purpose of this exercise is to help clients use a method known as "Active Constructive Responding" (ACR) to improve and strengthen their relationships.

Suggestions for Use

This exercise can be used with any clients who would like to have more satisfying relationships. It may be particularly helpful with couples. As part of this exercise, help clients to distinguish between different types of responding: Active and Destructive, Passive and Destructive, Passive and Constructive, and Active and Constructive. Examples of each are given in the exercise itself. It is also important to have clients practice Active Constructive Responding (ACR) so that it becomes part of their everyday conversations.

Exercise

For this exercise, please complete each of the following sections.

1. Let's first learn about the different types of responses. Below are examples of situations in which a person shares news with another. What follows are different ways that the person who hears the news might respond.

   - Active and Destructive

     Statement: *I just got a promotion and I've only been working for the company for a year!*

     Response: *Sounds like a lot of work to me. I wouldn't want that kind of responsibility.*

   - Passive and Destructive

     Statement: *I got my project done! It took a little longer than expected but I'm really happy with the outcome.*

     Response: *Who's picking up the dry cleaning?*

   - Passive and Constructive

     Statement: *I really had a great day at work. I feel wonderful!*

     Response: *That's great.*

   - Active and Constructive

     Statement: *I feel like things are finally turning around for me. Both job interviews went well today.*

     Response: *That's terrific! I'd love to hear about the interviews. What do you say we grab a cup of coffee and chat?*

   What was your reaction to each of the ways of responding? Perhaps you can even recall a time when you responded in one or more of the ways listed. It is clear that the first two types of response can prove invalidating and, in some cases, disrespectful to the person sharing the good news. They also convey disinterest, self-centeredness, and lack of interest.

The third type is a reasonable one; however, it does not encourage further conversation. More importantly, it does allow the person sharing the news an opportunity to fully experience the effects of positive emotion in the presence of another person. So this kind of response is more neutral than positive because there is no active component to it.

The fourth type of response is both active and constructive. In ACR, we are acknowledging and validating *and* creating an opportunity to share in the positive experience of the person bearing the news. Beyond this, ACR sends an important message: "I care about you and what happens to you. Please tell me about what is important to you so I can share in that experience." ACR is not about over-responding or candy-coating things. It is a genuine response to another's positive experience.

ACR should also be accompanied by nonverbal behaviors that are consistent with the verbal response. For example, an ACR response could include eye contact, a touch to the other person's hand, a smile, and so on. Incongruent nonverbal responses might include arms folded, sighing, a subdued body posture, and the like. In other words, what is conveyed nonverbally should be consistent with what is stated verbally. ACR includes both verbal and nonverbal actions. With these forms of communication in sync, ACR can help build stronger relationships.

2. Now, let's practice. For each of the following statements, write a statement using ACR.

   Statement: *I can't believe I got an "A" on my final exam.*
   - My Response: _____
   _____

   Statement: *I just heard that my sister is going to have a baby. I'm going to be an aunt!*
   - My Response: _____
   _____

   Statement: *I just finished my first workout to try to lose weight. I know it's only one but I'm glad I finally did something good for my body.*
   - My Response: _____
   _____

   Statement: *I got the job transfer I hoped for. It will be sad to leave my hometown but it is the kind of opportunity I have been dreaming of.*
   - My Response: _____
   _____

   Statement: *I just received preapproval to buy a new home!*
   - My Response: _____
   _____

3. For the next week, practice ACR in your relationships. If applicable, talk with your therapist about the results of using ACR.

References

Gable, S. L., & Poore, J. (2008). Which thoughts count? Algorithms for evaluating satisfaction in relationships. *Psychological Science, 19*(10), 1030–1036.

Gable, S. L., Reis, H. T., Impett, E., & Asher, E. R. (2004). What do you do when things go right? The intrapersonal and interpersonal benefits of sharing positive events. *Journal of Personality and Social Psychology, 87*, 228–245.

Positive Coping

Overview

We often use Positive Psychology and solution-oriented methods to solve problems, but the purpose of this exercise is to use them to explore and highlight clients' use of more positive coping strategies (Bertolino & O'Hanlon, 2002). Most clients have a range of responses and coping strategies when confronted with stress and problems. The purpose of this exercise is to help clients discover, highlight, and encourage their best coping methods.

Suggestions for Use

This exercise, for therapists, is designed to highlight for the client and the therapist, the existence of better coping strategies in clients' lives. It is also designed to support the client in using these better strategies more often, sometimes just by highlighting them and therefore having clients notice them, and at other times by actively encouraging clients to use them more regularly.

Exercise

Here are some sample questions for exploring and supporting positive coping strategies. Create your own based on these models and personalized to your client's circumstances and sensibilities. If it helps, write a few of your clients' responses to the questions in the space provided.

- How did you deal with that? Was that different for you? Did that feel better or work better?

_____

_____

_____

_____

_____

_____

- Wow! You didn't freak out, but sat down and wrote out your feelings. That sounds like it worked better than what you did the last time this happened. How did you manage that? And do you think you will be able to do that if something like this happens again?

_____

_____

_____

_____

_____

_____

- You stayed calm when your mother yelled at you. How did you manage to stay calm? Did you like that way of dealing with it better? Did it get a different response from your mother or just help you?

_____

_____

_____

_____

- Instead of cutting yourself, you called a friend. What got you to think of that and do it?

_____

_____

_____

_____

_____

_____

Reference

Bertolino, B., & O'Hanlon, B. (2010). *Collaborative, competency-based counseling and therapy.* Boston, MA: Allyn & Bacon.

Positive Pre-Session Change

Overview

Our colleague Michele Weiner-Davis (Weiner-Davis, De Shazer, & Gingerich, 1987) conducted a study with some colleagues in which she investigated what she called "pre-treatment change." This is the notion that clients have often made positive changes before arriving at a therapist's office or the treatment center. But because we rarely ask about those changes, we may inadvertently miss them or undo that progress by focusing on asking about the problems without exploring these changes they have made prior to arriving.

The study found that asking about such positive pre-session changes resulted in 66% of the clients reporting such positive pre-treatment change in the first session (and even more clients in subsequent sessions recalled something they reported after the initial results were compiled). A replication study (Lawson, 1994) found that 61% of clients reported positive pre-treatment changes.

When such changes are reported, it can make the therapist's task much easier. The purpose of this exercise is to explore for these changes, and then ask clients what they would need to do to keep these positive changes going. The late Milton Erickson used to say that making change happen can be like getting a snowball rolling down a snowy hill. Once it is started, it can just pick up momentum and size as it keeps rolling along downhill. Because the clients have already started the ball rolling, the therapist might only have to keep it rolling and encourage it to pick up speed and size.

Suggestions for Use

Interestingly, another analysis (McKeel & Weiner-Davis, 1995) discovered that when therapists asked the pre-session change questions in a way that presupposed that pretreatment change hadn't happened, 67% of them did not report positive pretreatment change. So be careful about how you ask the questions and investigate this area. Your sense of positive expectancy might really affect the results you get with this method.

This exercise, for therapists, is designed to highlight for the client and the therapist, the existence of positive pretreatment change in clients' lives. It is also designed to support the client in keeping these changes going by actively encouraging clients to use them more in the future.

Exercise

Here are some sample questions and statements for exploring and supporting positive pretreatment change. Create your own based on these models and personalized to your client's circumstances and sensibilities. It may be helpful to write your client's responses to refer back to at a later time.

- I have noticed that many people have already made some good changes before they come in for their first session. Have you noticed that things have gotten any better in any area related to the problem recently or since you made the appointment? If so, what?

_____

_____

_____

_____

_____

_____

• [*If positive pretreatment change is reported*] How could you keep that good change going or expand it even further? How do you explain that this good change happened? Anything you did to make it happen or help it along?

_____

_____

_____

_____

_____

References

Lawson, D. (1994). Identifying pretreatment change. *Journal of Counseling and Development, 72,* 244–248.

McKeel, A. J., & Weiner-Davis, M. (1995). *Presuppositional questions and pretreatment change: A further analysis.* Unpublished manuscript.

Weiner-Davis, M., De Shazer, S., and Gingerich, W. J. (1987). Building on pretreatment change to construct the therapeutic solution. *Journal of Marital and Family Therapy, 13*(4), 359–363.

Additional Resources

Bertolino, B. (2010). *Strengths-based engagement and practice: Creating effective helping relationships.* Boston, MA: Allyn & Bacon.

O'Hanlon, W., & Weiner-Davis, M. (1988/2003). *In search of solutions: A new direction in psychotherapy.* New York: W.W. Norton.

On a Good Note

Overview

Throughout the history of psychotherapy, the primary focus has been on problems, pathology, and deficits. This makes sense in that most people begin therapy with some form of distress that they would like to get rid of or at least alleviate minimally. The "problem" with an almost exclusive focus on problems is that people can actually feel worse than they did before they began therapy. Because what we focus on tends to grow and expand, problems can seem to become bigger as more and more focus is placed on them. The purpose of this exercise is to offer the element of possibility in different forms of activities that tend to be primarily problem focused, thus leaving clients with an increased sense of hope and on a good note.

Suggestions for Use

This is an exercise to be completed by therapists, and the process can be used for all clients. It is well-suited to those instances when assessments, information-gathering processes, or other activities focus substantially on problems. In such cases, clients may leave interactions feeling worse than they did before they began. Even if conversations involve lengthy discussion of problems, it is important to leave clients on a good note. This exercise can help to inject a sense of hope into these types of situations. This process can be used at any point in therapy.

Exercise

1. As a therapist, begin by making a list of the different types of information-gathering tools you use. This can include assessments, questionnaires, forms, etc. Write the name of each information-gathering tool you use on the first line of the space provided below. Then, on the second line, briefly describe the purpose of each tool.

   Name of Tool:

   Purpose: _____

   +: _____

   Name of Tool: _____

   Purpose: _____

   +: _____

   Name of Tool: _____

   Purpose: _____

   +:_____

   Name of Tool: _____

   Purpose: _____

   +: _____

Name of Tool: _____

Purpose: _____

+: _____

2. Next to the "+" sign under each tool in Step 1, think of one way that as a therapist you can inject the element of possibility, hope, or optimism into the use of the measure. Write your ideas in the spaces provided. Examples are given below.

Name of Tool: *Intake Evaluation Form*

Purpose: *Gather demographic information; identify problems*

+:   *Ask questions about when problems seem more manageable; focus on what the client has done to keep problems from getting worse.*

Name of Tool: *Substance Use/Abuse Assessment*

Purpose: *Identify drugs of choice; determine level of use/abuse*

+:   *Ask questions about times when the client has remained abstinent (for any length of time), including how the client was able to do that and what he (she) specifically did.*

3. For this last part, take a moment to think about how your sessions or interaction typically come to a close. What kind of message do you leave with the client? Think of a way you can end your sessions in the future that will increase your clients' sense of hope and optimism. Write your idea in the space provided. Examples are given below.

Example: *Thank you for describing to me the challenges you are facing. I admire you for taking action to improve things in your life. Just coming here is a big step and one that some might never take. We will build on that strength as well as others you have as we go along.*
Example: *I'm really impressed with the strength you have shown to face the challenges you have had throughout your life. I'm looking forward to working with you.*
Note: It is important that your responses are genuine. Don't be overly dramatic or try to candy-coat things. This can come across as insensitive and feel invalidating to clients. Speak to the strengths and exceptions that the client has exhibited and highlight those in conversation.

_____

_____

_____

_____

_____

_____

My Mission

Overview

As therapists we become indoctrinated by theories and ideas that shape our practice. Over time these theories can take on a life of their own and become representations of what we believe about people and change. The downside of this is that without knowing, these mission statements can influence what we do and how we do it in therapy. The purpose of this exercise is to create a mission statement that reflects what you stand for as a clinician.

Suggestions for Use

This exercise is for therapists. A few years ago, Bill and I (Bob) were working on a project when one of the discussions turned to that of "mission" statements. We talked about what we wanted to stand for as therapists. We had both been trained in various models and had written about some specific movements as well. But when it came to developing a mission statement, none of these factors weighed in. In fact, in the end what we wrote as our mission statement had no connection with any theoretical persuasion. Our statement was: "We stand for those approaches that are respectful and effective and are opposed to those that are disrespectful and ineffective." This is a very general statement from which we have since derived more specific statements in our own practices; however, it was a good start for us. The aim of this exercise is to help you as a therapist to develop a mission statement.

Exercise

1. For this exercise, begin by making a list of the adjectives that capture the essence of your work. If you are just starting out as a therapist, think of words that you would use to describe what you want for your future clients. Please write your responses in the space provided.

Drawing on your list of words in Step 1, compose a statement that reflects what you stand for as a clinician. This statement can include what you hope for your clients, how you think about or approach helping your clients, and so on. Don't worry about "getting it right." The idea is to generate a starting point.

_____

_____

3. Take a break for a day or two and let what you have written sit. Then, revisit your mission statement and tweak it as you see fit. Allow yourself the time to think about each revision. When you can look at your mission statement and not make any further changes, ask two or more trusted colleagues for their feedback. You might also consider reviewing others' mission statements.
4. When you are satisfied, write your mission statement below and "Go Public" by posting it in your office, on your letterhead, website, and so on.

Mission Statement:

_____

_____

_____

_____

_____

_____

7

Income, Volunteerism, and Exercise

In this chapter you will find the final three elements of our P.O.S.I.T.I.V.E. framework. We first examine the relationship between money (income) and happiness and well-being. To do this we explore some myths as well as some realities. Basically, we tell you that money doesn't make you happy except when it does. Knowing when it does and doesn't can help keep things in perspective. Next, we examine the relationship between giving of oneself (volunteerism) and happiness or life satisfaction. And finally, we include the physical (movement and exercise) and its relationship to happiness, depression, and well-being.

Random Acts of Kindness

Overview

Life satisfaction was shown in one study (Williams, Haber, Weaver, & Freeman, 1998) to increase 24% with the level of altruistic activity in a person's life. The data are so compelling regarding the benefits of doing nice things for other people on one's happiness levels that Laura King, a Positive Psychology researcher, is quoted as saying, "People who want to live a more fulfilling life should quit reading self-help books and start helping others" (quoted in Biswas-Diener & Dean, 2007, p. 110).

One of our favorite books on this subject is an old one, but a gem. David Dunn's (1988) *Try Giving Yourself Away* was written (under a pseudonym) by a successful businessman in 1947. It has remained in print since then due to its cadre of hard-core fans. In it, Dunn gives some simple and moving thoughts about the value of daily giving to others and the benefits for one's own life of doing so. Long before the phrase "random acts of kindness" entered our lexicon, Dunn was advocating this as a way to a happier and more satisfying life.

This exercise is about giving. Although it may seem counterintuitive to think that giving to others can make one happier, perhaps that is because we are social beings and are hard-wired to help the group succeed. It works nonetheless. Of course, one cannot give in order to be happier. One must genuinely give without expecting anything in return to reap the benefits.

Suggestions for Use

For this set of activities, we have borrowed liberally from Dunn. He spent many years compiling a list of random acts of kindness that anyone could do for others. This exercise is designed to help people take the focus off themselves and to give for the sake of giving. Most of these activities do not cost anything. And we recommend, as does Dunn in his short book, that if possible, this giving is done anonymously. These activities can be done by either therapist or client.

Here are Dunn's guidelines for giving you might share with your clients:

Develop a habit of giving your kindness or compliments:
- Start as early in the day as you can.
- Find little ways of giving.
- Give with no thought of reward or even appreciation/recognition.
- Be a model of giving for the selfish, the suspicious, or the cynical.

- Make your appreciation to someone more in-depth by getting specific about what you appreciated about them or what they did.
- Give away surplus things you have that are just sitting there.
- Contribute to your friends, your family, your neighbors, your city, and your organizations.
- Give anonymously.
- Receive graciously when you are given a gift or kindness by someone.

Dunn also offers a suggestion that can "multiply your gift by three" by

- The generous and authentic spirit with which you give
- The timeliness of your gift
- Your enthusiasm when offering the gift

Exercise

Make a plan and an effort to do at least one thing each day for someone else. These do not have to be big things or expensive. At the end of one week, check in with yourself and decide whether you will continue this exercise for the next week. Continue until you die if it works for you.

Here is a list, derived and adapted from David Dunn's book (1947/1988), *Try Giving Yourself Away*, which we recommend you read if you get a chance.

- Take a moment to write a letter or card to someone.
- Park at a distance from the front door in whatever parking lot you use to give others closer spaces (this might even help you get a little more exercise and get healthier).
- Leave a five-dollar bill in a returned library book.
- Start your day by finding someone to whom you can give a compliment as soon as you can.
- Notice and say something nice about someone's appearance.
- Offer someone who looks like they are in a hurry your place in a long line.
- Give credit to someone else on a joint project.
- Encourage someone who is discouraged.
- Offer someone who is doubting himself (herself) your faith in their abilities.
- Offer to take an elderly or disabled person shopping or to a medical appointment.
- Offer to baby-sit for harried and stressed parents.
- Help a friend clean out a disorganized or messy closet, garage, or drawer.
- Give away something that you no longer use to someone you think might be able to use and benefit from it.
- Offer a smile to someone each day.
- Express your appreciation to someone who offers you a small kindness.

Add to this list in your own creative ways.

We leave you with a quotation from Winston Churchill:

"We make a living by what we get. But we make a life by what we give."

References

Biswas-Diener, R., & Dean, B. (2007). *Positive psychology coaching*. New York, NY: Wiley.

Dunn, D. (1947/1988). *Try giving yourself away*. Louisville, KY: Updegraff Press.

Williams, A., Haber, D., Weaver, G., & Freeman, J. (1998). Altruistic activity. *Activities, Adaptation, and Aging, 22,* 31.

The Positive Deviant in You

Overview

In the "Introduction" to this book, we discussed the story of Jerry and Monique Sternin and the couple's efforts in the Save the Children campaign. The Sternins identified "positive deviants"—or "PDs," as they were called—in communities in Vietnam in which there were high levels of malnutrition among children (Pascale, Sternin, & Sternin, 2010). PDs were parents who, despite the challenges of poverty and a 65% rate of malnutrition among children, had managed to keep their own children at a healthy weight. Through the careful study of these PDSs, subtle yet influential practices were identified that were associated with better-nourished children. The Sternins were then able to assist in the dissemination of these practices. These efforts ultimately contributed to decreased rates of malnutrition of 65% to 85% in every village the couple visited. The purpose of this exercise is to help clients identify efforts and actions that may run counter to popular thought but nonetheless positively affect their lives or the lives of others.

Suggestions for Use

This exercise involves exploring the Positive Deviant or "Outlier" in clients. The concept of the "Outlier" has been popularized (Gladwell, 2008) in the mainstream literature as those persons who fall outside the mainstream or some established norm and positively change the world through their actions. For this exercise we are encouraging positive deviance in ways that contribute to changes that extend beyond clients' immediate lives. This exercise is applicable to all clients.

Exercise

For this exercise, have clients complete the following steps.

1. Think of a situation in which you responded to a concern in a relationship, your family, or community that was outside of popular, conventional, or mainstream thought and how that response positively influenced the eventual outcome of the situation. Describe what you did in the space below.

   _____

   _____

   _____

   _____

2. What specifically was different or out of the ordinary about what you did—about your response?

   _____

   _____

   _____

   _____

3. Next, describe a situation or concern with which you believe you could make a positive "splash" in your community or region. Be sure what you describe is something that has the potential to positively benefit others.

_____

_____

_____

_____

4. What is most compelling about this situation or problem? What interests you about it?

_____

_____

_____

_____

5. How is the way you conceptualize the situation or concern different from the status quo?

_____

_____

_____

_____

6. What is a first step you can take to begin to positively influence the situation or concern?

_____

_____

_____

_____

7. Take the step you described in Step 6 and report about your experience.

_____

_____

_____

_____

8. Plan your next steps and monitor how your positive deviance influences a change in the situation or concern you described. Do your best to stay the course and focus on those things that will benefit others and contribute to changes in the world around you.

References

Gladwell, M. (2008). *Outliers: The story of success*. New York: Little, Brown and Company.
Pascale, R., Sternin, J., & Sternin, M. (2010). *The power of positive deviance: How unlikely innovators solve the world's toughest problems*. Boston, MA: Harvard Business Press.

Moving Out of Depression 1: Walking Sessions

Overview

A meta-analysis done by Sin and Lyubomirsky (2009) of 50+ Positive Psychology interventions with more than 4,000 individuals revealed that positive psychology interventions do indeed significantly enhance well-being and decrease depressive symptoms. So we know we can make a difference in people's depression levels, which of course, will typically increase their happiness levels.

In this exercise we focus on one specific aspect of helping people out of depression that may perhaps be surprising. There has been a raft of research performed showing that exercise is a promising activity for relieving depression. Our favorite is the SMILE (Standard Medical Intervention and Long Term Exercise) study (Blumenthal et al., 2007). In this study, 156 adults diagnosed with Major Depressive Disorder were randomly assigned to one of three groups:

1. A group that received standard anti-depressant treatment (with Zoloft).
2. An exercise-only group. Exercise consisted of brisk walking, jogging, or stationary bicycle riding three times a week (consisting of a 10-minute warm-up; 30 minutes of aerobic exercise; followed by a 5-minute cool-down).
3. A combined exercise and anti-depressant treatment group. These subjects did the same exercise regimen as the exercise group above, but also received standard Zoloft treatment.

The preliminary results were gratifying. At the end of four months of these interventions, 60% to 70% of the participants were "vastly improved" or "symptom-free" in all three conditions. The follow-up results may be somewhat unexpected. At 10 months, 38% of Zoloft condition subjects had recurrence of their major depression. Only 31% of the combined condition had recurrence. But, astoundingly, only 8% of the exercise-only group had recurrence (and people who continued to exercise were even less likely as a group to have recurrence). How much exercise mattered: Every 50 minutes of exercise per week was correlated with a 50% drop in depression levels.

What explains such results? Most would have predicted that the combined condition would have yielded superior results. The experimenters do not know, but there are a few factors that might explain the results. One is that the exercise-only condition subjects knew that the positive results had come solely from their own efforts. Perhaps that empowered them and furthered the results.

But another explanation comes from emerging new understandings of depression and the new brain science. With the discovery in the past quarter of a century of brain plasticity and neurogenesis (new brain and neuronal growth) in adults, this brain growth (rather than lack of it) might be one of the causes of depression. And exercise is one of the best ways to restart brain growth (Ratey, 2008).

This new hypothesis about the cause of depression is called the Neurogenic/Neuroatrophy Hypothesis of Depression. So far, evidence for the theory is sketchy. However, recent findings show a pattern that fits with the theory:

- Stress, which plays a key role in triggering depression, suppresses neurogenesis in the hippocampus.
- Antidepressants, on the other hand, encourage the birth of new brain cells.
- Animals must take antidepressants for two or three weeks before they bump up the birth rate of brain cells, and the cells take maybe another two weeks to start functioning. That's consistent with the lag time that antidepressants show before they lift mood in people.
- If an antidepressant is given during a period of chronic stress, it prevents the decline in neurogenesis that normally occurs.
- Exercise, which combats depression in people, also promotes neurogenesis in the hippocampus.

- So does electroconvulsive therapy, popularly known as shock treatment, which works in human cases of severe depression.
- Scientists have also found evidence that the hippocampus shrinks in people who have had long-standing depression.

Consider these recent research findings:

- Even small amounts of exercise can make a difference right away. Cognitive flexibility improves after just one 35-minute treadmill session at either 60% or 70% of maximum heart rate (Netz, Tomer, Axelrad, Argov, & Inbar, 2007).
- After a month on the running wheel, mice doubled the number of new neurons in the hippocampus (Van Praag, McIntosh, Wincour, & Grady, 2005).
- Exercise stimulates the production and release of growth factor BDNF (Brain-Derived Neurotrophic Factor), which can lead to new neurons and neuronal connections (Vaynman & Gomez-Pinilla, 2005).

To restart brain growth in depressed people, it is important to get them moving. Regular aerobic exercise would be ideal, but because that is not a realistic option with most depressed clients (at least at first), the activity suggested here would get things started in the right direction.

Suggestions for Use

This activity is primarily for clients who suffer from mild to severe forms of depression. Because depression is one known factor that decreases people's happiness over longer periods of time, alleviating depression, even slightly, can increase felt happiness and subjective well-being.

Exercise

Because many depressed clients will have trouble getting themselves moving, your task, as the therapist, is to get them moving by making your next few sessions "walking sessions." That is, after discussing it with your client, conduct your session while walking. If weather permits, walk near your office. If not, find an indoor setting, like a shopping mall, to do the walking session. If absolutely necessary and you find that neither of those options work, walk around your office with your client while doing the session.

References

Blumenthal, J. A., Babyak, M. A., Doraiswamy, P. M., Watkins, L., Hoffman, B. M., Barbour, K. A., Herman, S., Craighead, W. E., Brosse, A. L., Waugh, R., Hinderliter, A., & Sherwood, A. (2007). Exercise and pharmacotherapy in the treatment of major depressive disorder. *Psychosomatic Medicine, 69,* 587–596.

Netz, Y., Tomer, R., Axelrad, S., Argov, E., & Inbar, O. (2007). The effect of a single aerobic session on cognitive flexibility in late middle-aged adults. *International Journal of Sports Medicine, 28,* 82–87.

Ratey, J. (2008). *Spark: The revolutionary new science of exercise and the brain.* New York: Little Brown.

Sin, N., & Lyubomirsky, S. (2009). Enhancing well-being and alleviating depression with positive psychology interventions: A practice-friendly meta-analysis. *Journal of Clinical Psychology: In Session, 65,* 467–487.

Van Praag, H., McIntosh, A. R., Wincour, G., & Grady, C. L. (2005). Running increases cell proliferation and neurogenesis in the adult mouse dentate gyrus. *Nature Neuroscience, 2*(3), 266–270.

Vaynman, S., & Gomez-Pinilla, F. (2005). License to run: Exercise impacts functional plasticity in the intact and injured central nervous system by using neurotrophins. *Neurorehabilitation and Neural Repair, 19*(4), 283–295.

Moving Out of Depression 2 Baby Steps

Overview

We have covered some of the research and rationale for using movement and exercise to help people shift their depressive experience. One piece of good news is that a recent set of studies found that, even clients who are "treatment resistant" for antidepressants, exercise and movement can help. One study (Trivedi, Greer, Grannemann, Chambliss, & Jordan, 2006) found that people who participated in moderately intense aerobics, such as exercising on a treadmill or stationary bicycle—whether it was for three or five days per week—experienced a decline in depressive symptoms by an average of 47% after 12 weeks. Those in the low-intensity exercise groups showed a 30% reduction in symptoms. Exercise also helped people who were unresponsive to antidepressant medications (Dunn et al., 2005).

And it seems that depressed people can benefit the most from exercise and movement. If one is not depressed, one may not feel happier and less depressed after exercising. But University of Virginia researcher Robert Brown (Brown, Ramirez, & Taub, 1978) found that exercise had the most profound mood-lifting effect on people who were depressed and the effect increased with the amount of exercise. The study also found reductions in anger and anxiety through exercise.

A Purdue University study (Lobstein, Mosbacher, & Ismail, 1983) found that middle-aged runners who had been running three to five times a week for 3 to 10 years were markedly less depressed than a matched comparison group. Now, of course, we don't know from this study whether less depressed people tend to be runners or if running for that long helped prevent or lift depression. But given the preponderance of evidence, it would be prudent to get our depressed clients moving. This exercise is designed to do just that.

Suggestions for Use

This activity is primarily for clients who suffer from mild to severe forms of depression. The point of the activity is to get depressed clients moving, even a little.

Exercise

Because many depressed clients will have trouble getting themselves moving, talk to them about starting out with small steps. Ask them to walk a little more each day. Perhaps the first day, they will find it hard to walk from the bed to the living room; but if they commit to adding a little movement each day, before long, they may be walking around the block. Then encourage them to walk around the block twice each day. And so on. Encourage them to use every chance they can to get moving, but to keep each step small so they can achieve it and don't become discouraged or overwhelmed.

If you discover that they are pushing themselves too much or too fast, talk to your clients about restraint. Of course, your clients are the ultimate experts on their own capacities and what is right for them, so don't impose this restraint—but do raise the issue as a concern if appropriate.

References

Brown, R. S., Ramirez, D., & Taub, J. (1978). The prescription of exercise for depression. *Physician and Sportsmedicine, 6,* 35–45.

Dunn, A., Madhukar, H. Trivedi, M., Kampert, J. B., Clark, C. G., & Chambliss, H. (2005). Exercise treatment for depression: Efficacy and dose response. *American Journal of Preventive Medicine, 28*(1), 1–8.

Lobstein, D. D., Mosbacher, B. J., & Ismail, A. H. (1983). Depression as a powerful discriminator between physically active and sedentary middle-aged men. *Journal of Psychosomatic Medicine, 27*(1), 69–76.

Trivedi, M. H., Greer, T. L., Grannemann, B. D., Chambliss, H. O., & Jordan, A. N. (2006). Exercise as an augmentation strategy for treatment of major depression. *Journal of Psychiatric Practice, 12*(4), 205–213.

Walking Out of Anxiety

Overview

We should not leave the physical out of our survey. We are, after all, physical beings, with bodies that affect our minds (and vice versa). We came across evidence that a relatively small amount of physical activity can reduce levels of anxiety and, because anxiety is one of those thieves of happiness and subjective well-being, we thought we would include it. Most Positive Psychology literature does not touch on this area, but for the sake of completeness, we are including it. This exercise, therefore, is about clients and physical activity.

One study (Antunes, Stella, Santos, Bueno, & De Mello, 2005) found that seniors who had never exercised before experienced a mood-lifting effect (less depression and anxiety and better reported quality of life) from regular aerobic exercise (three times per week on alternate days for six months). Another study (Moses, Steptoe, Mathews, & Edwards, 1989) compared the effects of exercising at 60% of maximum heart rate with that at 70% to 75% (three times per week) over 10 weeks; the study showed significant reductions in trait anxiety for the 60% group and no reductions for the 70% to 75% group. It seems for anxiety that keeping the exercise at reasonable levels is better for relieving anxiety.

Norwegian psychiatrist Egil Martinsen (Martinsen, Hoffart, & Solberg, 1989) did a study that showed the effects of exercise on anxiety. In this study, 36 anxiety disorder patients voluntarily committed themselves to a hospital for eight weeks. All had failed to benefit from outpatient treatment and agreed to stop all anti-anxiety medication during this hospital stay. During their stay, all patients did an hour of aerobic exercise five days a week for the eight weeks. At the end of that time, anxiety scores decreased for all patients (except those with social anxiety). One-year follow-up showed that those with Generalized Anxiety Disorder and agoraphobia without panic attacks maintained treatment gains.

Suggestions for Use

This exercise is primarily for clients who suffer from either trait anxiety (those clients who are generally anxious) or state anxiety (more transient experiences of anxiety).

Exercise

For this exercise, mention the aforementioned research to your client and talk about his (her) thoughts on it. Next, suggest that the client try a short course of regular walking or more vigorous aerobic exercise (if it is appropriate and they are willing). Encourage the client to start small; studies show that as little as 10 to 15 minutes a day might be enough to decrease anxiety levels in a noticeable way.

Check back with your client and assess the results of this activity. Adjust as necessary.

References

Antunes, H. K. M., Stella, S. G., Santos, R. F., Bueno, O. F. A., & De Mello, M. T. (2005). *Revista Brasileira de Psiquiatria, 27*(4), 266–271.

Martinsen, E. W., Hoffart, A., & Solberg, Ø. Y. (1989). Aerobic and non-aerobic forms of exercise in the treatment of anxiety disorders. *Stress Medicine, 5*(2), 115–120.

Moses, J., Steptoe, A., Mathews, A., & Edwards, S. (1989). The effects of exercise training on mental well being in the normal population. *Journal of Psychosomatic Research, 33*(1), 47–61.

Stepping off the Treadmill

Overview

One of the challenges to happiness exists in the gap between what people think will make them happy and what actually does make them happy. We just aren't very good at predicting what will bring us happiness. The tendency of a person to remain at a relatively stable level of happiness despite changes in fortune or the achievement of major goals is referred to as the "hedonic treadmill." As people make more money, expectations and desires rise in tandem, but this does not result in a permanent gain in happiness. The purpose of this exercise is to help clients step off the hedonic treadmill and focus more on those things that will bring about enduring happiness.

Suggestions for Use

This exercise is for all clients, particularly those who focus on the accumulation of more "things" such as more money, bigger homes, and so on. One way to introduce the idea of the hedonic treadmill is by identifying those things that clients assumed would make them happier in the long run and did provide a brief boost, but faded shortly thereafter. Then encourage things that are likely to contribute to sustained happiness. It is important to make the distinction that things such as more money *can* make people happier if those things are used to do the things that really do make people happier. For example, if an increase in wealth gives people freedom to spend more time with loved ones, to help or give to others, to reduce the number of sources of stress around them, or to support artistic or scientific pursuits, then that happiness is more likely to last.

Exercise

1. Begin this exercise by placing a check in the box (indicated by the "+" sign) next to the "things" that you have had increases in (i.e., gained more of or experienced a positive change with) and that have positively influenced your level of happiness over the past year:

	+	Months	What Specifically?
Money/wealth			
Electronic goods			
Vehicles			
Boats/campers/RVs			
Property			
Spirituality			
Intelligence			
Social relationships (# of contacts per month)			
Satisfaction with work			
Intimate/love relationships			
Personal freedom			
Volunteering			
Subjective sense of health			
Sense of humor			

2. Using the same set of items, write (in number of months, in the "months" column) how long the increase in happiness has continued (i.e., 1 month, 11 months, etc.).
3. Take a moment to review your indications. Which of the items you checked show an increase in happiness beyond one month? Three months? Six months?
4. For the items that you have experienced increases in happiness for a minimum of three months, write what specifically contributed to that increase (e.g., a new car, more friends, etc.) in the rightmost column ("What Specifically?"). What do you notice about the things that contributed to your increase in happiness?
5. Research to date has shown that the top seven items do not typically lead to sustained increases in happiness, whereas the second grouping of seven items do individually, in general, contribute to higher, longer-term levels of happiness. Of course, the degree of influence will depend on the person.
6. Take a look at the things on your list that either went unchecked or did not contribute to increases in happiness beyond a month or so. Consider how you might make adjustments in your life to work more toward the things that seem to increase happiness in the long run versus those that keep you on the "hedonic treadmill." In the space below, write at least two things you might do differently over the next month to increase your activity among the second set of seven items. Be sure to keep your plans simple and "doable."

Plan 1

_____

_____

Plan 2

_____

_____

Additional Resource

Gilbert, D. (2006). *Stumbling on happiness*. New York: Vintage.

Simplification

Overview

The path to well-being has many inroads. One the most important—yet overlooked—inroads involves the simplification of those things that can take up a lot of time and energy, build stress, and leave people with less of "themselves" to go around. The purpose of this exercise is to help clients identify small but critical changes they can make to simplify their lives.

Suggestions for Use

This exercise is all for the client but may be particularly useful for those who seem to struggle with time management and report burning the "candle at both ends." The idea is to help clients identify everyday tasks that require large amounts of time, cause stress, and take away from time that could be spent on more satisfying and gratifying things.

Exercise

For this exercise, have client complete the following steps.

1. Make a list of the daily, weekly, and monthly tasks that require large amounts of time or contribute to higher levels of stress for you, or tasks that take away from time that could be spent on more enjoyable things in life.

Task   **Rank**

_____   _____
_____   _____
_____   _____
_____   _____
_____   _____
_____   _____
_____   _____
_____   _____
_____   _____
_____   _____

2. Next, rank the tasks you listed in Step 1 in the order of stress they bring to your life (i.e., "#1" contributes to the most stress and "#10" contributes to the least stress of the tasks listed).
3. Take the top three tasks on your list and think of one way that you could simplify each of them. Write the task you are addressing and the ideas you develop in the space provided below.

Task #1

_____

One thing I can do:

_____

Task #2

One thing I can do:

Task #3

One thing I can do:

To assist with this process, here are some general ideas to help you with considering changes might import into your life. Please keep in mind that general ideas should always have specific applications to truly make a difference for a person. In other words, do what works for you.

- Financial — For bills, consider using automated payments to simplify payment processes and decrease the time you spend on that task. This can also boost your well-being as you won't be thinking about paying bills as much.
- Let it go — If something is weighing on your mind, deal with it as soon as you can. Carrying around guilt or worry has implications for psychological and physical health. Make a plan to deal with the issue and let it go. If you need to make amends or reparation, make a plan to do so as soon as possible. Then spend your energy on those things that are better for you. Your well-being, relationships, and work/school performance can greatly improve for relieving your worries.
- Scheduling — Block out times that you will be unavailable so you can have brief periods of free time. Consider moving from a paper to an electronic method of scheduling such as a phone or online system. Just be sure to back up your schedule.
- Housework/chores — Put a calendar somewhere that is very visible. Identify specific tasks, chores, and areas of maintenance that need to be completed on a daily, weekly, or monthly basis. If you live with others, make sure each person knows his or her responsibilities. In your personal schedule list your responsibilities with other tasks and appointments.
- Rest — If you are constantly tired or overwhelmed, take brief breaks of 5 to 10 minutes to rest. Lay your head on your desk, practice taking deep breaths, listen to music, etc. Then reengage in your work. These brief periods of rest can reenergize you, help you be more creative, and give you peace of mind.
- Social — Schedule time to meet with friends and other social supports. Do not wait for the "right time." Schedule get-togethers just as you would schedule other appointments. Put them on your schedule and follow through with them. And don't cancel!
- Exercise — Build in time, each and every day, to exercise for at least 20 minutes. Be consistent and follow through. And don't let being tired deter you. You can benefit greatly from exercise when you are most tired! Exercise can give you more energy throughout your day to deal with the tasks that must be accomplished.
- Sleep — Establish a routine and get your sleep. Enough said.
- Meals — Plan as many meals as possible. Know where you are going to eat and, in general, what you are going to eat. If you are going to have the strength you need, when you need it, then it is important to ensure that you have the foods available that will provide you with the necessary nutrition and energy. Planning meals can reduce your everyday stress because you

will not have to worry about what you are going to eat. It can also relieve you of subsequent guilt from having settled for something you didn't want or didn't agree with your body in the first place.

4. With the extra time and reduced level of stress you will have, how will you be sure to use that time and extra energy in ways that benefit you and others? Be sure to give this some thought as it is very easy to replace tasks and work with other tasks and more work, which is counter to the purpose of simplifying to increase well-being.

5. Now, try one or more of the ideas you listed in Step 3 and report back on the results.

_____

_____

_____

_____

_____

Resource

Rath, R., & Harter, J. (2010). *Well-being: The five essential elements*. New York: Gallup Press.

Stopping Money Leaks

Overview

As mentioned in the "Introduction" money doesn't buy happiness, but the lack of money often buys unhappiness and stress. Many of our clients mismanage their money, sometimes because they are focused on their emotional, psychological, behavioral, and relational issues, sometimes because they never developed good financial hygiene. One of the most common sources of money problems is *money leakage*. This is when people either spend money unnecessarily or fail to stop money-draining fees and activities. This exercise is about stopping these kinds of leaks.

Let's first examine the typical money leaks people have:

Late fees: These are fees that are assessed because people pay their bills late.
Indulgent expenses: These are things people spend money on to reduce stress or reward themselves for being so busy or working so hard.
Impulse buys: These are purchases made without doing the necessary research to ensure this is the right product or service or it is the best value.
Interest charges: Paying banks fees for using their money, through credit cards, check cashing fees, and so on.
No savings/cushion: This is when people have no savings and have to forgo bargains or pay extra (for example, charging an emergency automobile repair on a high-interest credit card they do not pay off right away) to do or buy something.

Suggestions for Use

Money, like politics and sex, can sometimes seem like a taboo subject, but it may be important to discuss this issue with clients because, if not addressed, it might be adding to clients' stress and therefore their unhappiness.

Obviously, do not be unhelpfully intrusive, but a gentle inquiry into this area might yield some insight into your client's money issues and you might be helpful in relieving some of their money-related stresses.

Exercise

Give your client a list like the one below. Have your client fill it out and discuss it with him (her) after he (she) returns it.

1. Late fees: Are you paying or do you pay any late fees on a regular basis?
   If so, what small steps could you take to reduce or eliminate future late fees? Is there anyone you could call on to help you with this?

   1. _____
   2. _____
   3. _____

2. Indulgent purchases: Are you buying yourself things for emotional reasons or rewarding yourself for working so hard and then having to stress about the money you spent on those purchases or work harder to pay for those indulgent purchases?

If so, what small steps could you take to reduce or eliminate this kind of spending, at least until you have a cushion or some savings built up and don't feel financial stress? Is there anyone you could call on to help you with this?

1. _____
2. _____
3. _____

3. Impulse buys: Are you buying things without researching them to ensure you are making wise purchases or getting the best value for your purchase?
   If so, what small steps could you take to reduce or eliminate impulse buying? Is there anyone you could call on to help you with this?

   1. _____
   2. _____
   3. _____

4. Interest charges: Are you paying or do you pay any interest charges (other than your standard first mortgage) on a regular basis?
   If so, what small steps could you take to reduce or eliminate interest charges? Is there anyone you could call on to help you with this?

   1. _____
   2. _____
   3. _____

5. No savings/cushion: Do you have at least one month's income saved as a cushion for emergencies?
   If not, what small steps could you take to put away one month's income? Is there anyone you could call on to help you with this?

   1. _____
   2. _____
   3. _____

These lists may lead to other money/financial stress or financial pattern discussions. Help clients sort out their money issues and develop financial health if appropriate. We suggest you have them read the book listed below if they need a reorientation regarding money, savings and spending.

Resource

Robins, V., & Dominguez, J., with Tilford, M. (2008). *Your money or your life: 9 steps to transforming your relationship with money and achieving financial independence.* New York: Penguin.

Can Money Make You Happy?

Overview

If you ask many people what would make them happier, they would say, "I would win the lottery." Or, "More money." Or "If I didn't have to work." But is it true? Does money make you happy? Would having more money make you more happy? The answer isn't a simple yes or no. It is both yes and no. This exercise is about making distinctions between what money can and cannot do in terms of levels of happiness.

First, recall the oft-cited research (Brickman, Coates, & Janoff-Bulman, 1978) that found that one year after winning the lottery, people's happiness levels return to where they were before the drastic change of circumstance. This is due to what has been called one's "happiness set point," a genetically or temperamentally influenced level of happiness and well-being that, if nothing happens to permanently change it, becomes the level around which most of us vary slightly and to which we return after the short ups and downs of life.

Second, consider the oft-cited fact (Layard, 2005) that happiness levels in the United States and other industrialized nations have not increased for the past 50 years, despite massive increases in real income for every income level. Approximately 45% of the wealthiest Americans report being very happy; 33% of the bottom quarter of income level people report being happy (and that also hasn't changed for the past 50 years).

However, if you look at the fact cited above, you will notice that more wealthy than less wealthy Americans report being happy. This seems to be due, in part, to comparing ourselves with others. If we win by the comparison, most of us will feel a little happier; if we lose by the comparison, most of us will feel a bit less happy. In addition, it appears that having a certain level of income and money does have a correlation with one's happiness level but after that level is reached, more income does not generally result in much more happiness.

Americans who earn $50,000 per year are much happier, in general, than those who earn $10,000 per year, but those who earn $5 million per year are not substantially happier than those who earn $100,000 per year. And people who live in poor countries are less happy than those who live in moderately wealthy countries; but those who live in moderately wealthy countries are not much happier than those who live in very wealthy countries. The level at which more money stops affecting happiness levels varies from country to country and over time, but it is somewhere between $2,000 per year and $75,000/ per year (Layard, 2005).

As Leo Rosten has quipped: "Money can't buy happiness, but neither can poverty."

Suggestions for Use

One way, then, to increase one's sense of satisfaction and well-being is to compare oneself to others who are not as well off. To keep this process from being too cruel, one could use people from the past as a comparison, and this is what the exercise in this section does. It can be done by either the therapist or the client.

Exercise

Make a list of all the things you have in your life that the richest person in the middle ages did not have. Think of all the work and hardship in your life that is spared due to these everyday luxuries and conveniences. We'll start you out.

- Indoor plumbing
- Hot and cold running water

- Refrigerator and freezer to keep food cool and fresh
- _____
- _____
- _____
- _____
- _____
- _____
- _____
- _____
- _____
- _____
- _____

After making this list, consider how often you take your basic wealth and luxury for granted and how, compared to people of the past, you are more pampered than most royalty were in past eras.

References

Brickman, P., Coates, D., & Janoff-Bulman, R. (1978). Lottery winners and accident victims: Is happiness relative? *Journal of Personality and Social Psychology, 36,* 917–927

Layard, R. (2005). *Happiness: Lessons from a new science.* New York: Penguin.

Additional Resources

Gilbert, D. (2006). *Stumbling on happiness.* New York: Vintage.

Lyubomirsky, S. (2007). *The how of happiness: A scientific approach to getting the life you want.* New York: Penguin.

Weiner, E. (2008). *The geography of bliss: One grump's search for the happiest places in the world.* New York: Hachette.

The Pleasure of Service

Overview

Pleasure and service are sometimes seen as two very different things. Pleasure usually equates to those things that provide immediate but short-term gratification. Service, on the other hand, is something that enhances or contributes to the lives of *others* and generally contributes longer experiences of happiness. The purpose of this exercise is twofold. The first is to compare the differences between pleasure and service. The second is to combine both pleasure and service. After all, why not enjoy the gift of helping others?

Suggestions for Use

This exercise is suited for all clients. Talk with the client about the differences between pleasure and service. You might explain that this exercise is to help better understand the short- and long-term effects of the two things, and to ultimately combine the two to achieve the "best of both worlds." This exercise will take a few weeks to a month to complete, so be sure to plan accordingly.

Exercise

Have the client begin by completing the following two steps.

1. Choose something that will likely make you feel better right away (e.g., going to favorite restaurant, buying something you want, etc.). In the space below, write what you did and the date you did it. Then, immediately after the act, assign a number between 1 and 10, in which 1 stands for very low and 10 stands for very high, that describes the level of happiness you achieved.
Date _____
What I Did _____
Immediate Rating (from 1 to 10) _____
Two weeks after the act, assign a number between 1 and 10, in which 1 stands for very low and 10 stands for very high, that describes the level of happiness you achieved.
Two-Week Rating (from 1 to 10) _____
2. Over the next week, do something to help a person in need, or do something service oriented in your community, or volunteer somewhere. In the space below, write what you did and the date you did it. Then, immediately after the service activity, assign a number between 1 and 10, in which 1 stands for very low and 10 stands for very high, that describes the level of happiness you achieved.
Date _____
What I Did _____
Immediate Rating (from 1 to 10) _____
Two weeks after the service activity, assign a number between 1 and 10, in which 1 stands for very low and 10 stands for very high, that describes the level of happiness you achieved.
Two-Week Rating (from 1 to 10) _____
3. Compare the ratings you assigned to both activities. For which activity was the Two-Week Rating higher? In most cases, the Two-Week Rating for the Service-Oriented Activity will be higher. This is because the act of helping others yields longer-term happiness.
4. For this last step we want to experience the best of both worlds—pleasure and service at the same time. The question is: What can you do to make a contribution to the lives of others and experience pleasure in doing it?

Think of an idea that will touch on both pleasure and service, and put it into action. Describe your plan in the space below and:
Assign an Immediate Rating of happiness (from 1 to 10) _____

_____

_____

_____

_____

_____

5. Talk about your experience with combining pleasure and service. What did you notice?

_____

_____

_____

_____

_____

At Two Weeks, Assign a Rating of Happiness (from 1 to 10) _____

6. What can you learn from this experience?

_____

_____

_____

_____

_____

Volunteers of America

Overview

We came across some intriguing and suggestive research (Stirman & Pennebaker, 2001) as we were preparing this book. About 300 poems from the early, middle, and late periods of nine suicidal poets and nine non-suicidal poets—from the 1800s to the present—were compared using a computer text analysis program, Linguistic Inquiry and Word Count (LIWC). Textual analysis of poets who committed suicide shows more use of the words "I," "me," and "mine," when compared with poets who died of natural causes.

This is a perfect lead-in to this exercise and topic. As we familiarized ourselves with the literature of Positive Psychology, one insight kept popping up here and there: Living a selfish life concerned with making oneself happy is rarely (if ever) the path to happiness and life satisfaction.

Humanitarian Albert Schweitzer said it well: "The only ones among you who will be really happy are those who will have sought and found how to serve."

A research summary prepared by Volunteer Ontario (Graff, 1991) found that volunteering has been shown to be associated with improvements in self-esteem, reductions in heart rates and blood pressure, increases in endorphin production, enhancement of immune systems, buffering of the impact of stress, and less social isolation.

Volunteering has even been associated with better survivor rates of older adults. A University of Michigan study by Stephanie Brown and colleagues (Brown, Nesse, Vinokur, & Smith, 2003) followed 423 older couples for five years and found that those who reported (unpaid) helping someone else even as little as once a year were between 40 and 60% less likely to die than those who reported not helping anyone else during the previous year. The help they gave was sometimes as simple as helping take care of grandchildren, or assisting family members in need, as well as volunteering.

A 20-year-long study (Pillemer, Fuller-Rowell, Reid, & Wells, 2010) followed more than 6,000 middle-aged Americans from the mid-1970s when they began their volunteer activities in ecological restoration projects, environmental stewardship programs, and environmental policy-making activities. In the mid-1990s they were evaluated as to their levels of physical activity, self-reported health, and depressive symptoms. After controlling for a number of factors, the researchers found that people who were involved in these volunteer activities were more active, healthier, and more optimistic and happier than those who were not involved in such activities.

We hope you get the point. Volunteering, despite the time and effort it takes, can be beneficial in providing meaning and well-being for the volunteer in addition to the direct social good it does. Giving may be better than receiving, as the old saying goes.

Suggestions for Use

This exercise is primarily for clients who are isolated or find their lives less meaningful than they would like.

Exercise

For this exercise, engage the client around the following idea:

- First, ask the client where he would volunteer if he chose to. What social plight moves him the most? Where have any of his friends, colleagues, or family members ever volunteered, and do any of those settings or causes interest him?

- If the client struggles to come up with any volunteer opportunities, have him (her) interview people he (she) knows or meets about the possibilities for volunteering. Have the client ask those people who have volunteered what the experience was like and why they volunteered.
- Then suggest that the client volunteer as much as is feasible for the next month and check back with you at the end of that time to process the experience and decide whether he (she) will continue with volunteering.

References

Brown, S., Nesse, R., Vinokur, A., & Smith, D. (2003). Providing social support may be more beneficial than receiving it: Results from a prospective study of mortality. *Psychological Science, 14,* 320–327.

Graff, L. (1991). *Volunteer for the health of it.* Etobicoke, Ontario: Volunteer Ontario.

Pillemer, K., Fuller-Rowell, T., Reid, M., & Wells, N. (2010). Environmental volunteering and health outcomes over a 20-year period. *The Gerontologist, 50,* 594–560.

Stirman, S.W., & Pennebaker, J. (2001). Word use in the poetry of suicidal and nonsuicidal poets. *Psychosomatic Medicine, 63,* 517–522.

(This) State of Mine

Overview

More and more research shows that levels of happiness and well-being vary throughout the world. Bill, for example, lives in a state (New Mexico) that is considered in the upper half of the well-being rankings. Bob's state of residence (Missouri), on the other hand, is in the bottom half (Gallup-Healthways Well-Being Index, January–December, 2009). Does this mean Bill is happier than Bob? That would be too simplistic a viewpoint. As we have learned throughout this book, there are, of course, many influences on well-being. The purpose of this exercise is to explore pathways to increase well-being for those clients—no matter the state.

Suggestions for Use

This exercise is set up for any client who resides in the United States and may have an interest in exploring ways of tapping into the factors that affect well-being in their areas of residence. This exercise can also be done with those clients who live outside the United States by locating well-being indices for other countries. A way of introducing this exercise is by talking with clients about what can be learned by the study of where people live.

Exercise

For this exercise, have the client explore the following areas:

• Take a moment to think about where you live, including the best and the not-so-good about your country, state, or city. In the space below, make a list of the positives and negatives.

+ _____   – _____

_____   _____

_____   _____

_____   _____

_____   _____

_____   _____

_____   _____

• Next, go to the Gallup-Healthways Well-Being Index (www.well-beingindex.com) and look up your state's ranking and write it in the space below.

State Ranking: _____

• Consider what you listed as positive and negatives in comparison to your state's ranking. What do you notice? Write your response in the space below.

_____

_____

_____

_____

- Next, consider the following questions:
  - What can you do to better tap into the positives that your state has to offer?
  - What can you do to better face the challenges faced by your state in terms achieving higher levels of well-being?
- Talk with or interview others who live around you and ask them the questions listed above.
- Talk with people from other states or countries who live in areas that have higher rankings of well-being than yours. Find out what these people identify as positive influences on well-being.
- In the space below, write what you can do to import one or more of the ideas you have learned from others—both local and distant—into your life, relationships, community, and state. In other words, write about how you can change your "state"!

_____

_____

_____

_____

_____

Remember, even seemingly little things can make big changes!

Reference

Gallup. (2008). *Gallup-Healthways Well-Being Index.* www.well-beingindex.com/

Additional Resources

Rath, R., & Harter, J. (2010). *Well-being: The five essential elements*. New York: Gallup Press.
Weiner, E. (2008). *The geography of bliss: One grump's search for the happiest places in the world*. New York: Hachette.

–8–

Summary and Sendoff

Although this book draws on research into happiness and subjective well-being, we haven't really discussed the nature of happiness and how it is measured in this research.

There are two main ways that happiness and subjective well-being are assessed. One is by contemporaneous measurements. The first of these methods involves beeping people randomly during their daily lives and asking them to rate their mood and sense of happiness or well-being at each of those moments. The other contemporaneous way is to measure such observables as brain waves, smiling, laughing, sociability, and heart rates.

The other way is to have people answer questions or place themselves on scales of happiness and well-being. They are asked questions such as, "Taking all things together, would you say you are very happy, quite happy, not very happy, or not at all happy?" and "All things considered, how satisfied are you with your life as a whole these days?" (You can find examples of this kind of survey at the World Values Survey website: http://www.worldvaluessurvey.org/index_surveys).

A variation on this method is used by the Gallop organization. They ask people to put themselves on the rung of a ladder, with each rung representing a progressively better life.

And then there is the distinction that measuring happiness or well-being or positive emotions measures one kind of thing—present experience—and asking people to assess their level of general happiness—their stories and ideas about their overall experience—are assessing very different things. And happiness seems to be different from subjective well-being.

Well, we'll leave those heady matters to the philosophers, academicians, and researchers while we plunge ahead. The philosopher José Ortega y Gasset once said, "Life is fired at us point blank." So is clinical work. We must do something when confronted with a suffering, upset client (or concerned relatives). No time for philosophical musings.

But we know what we are referring to when we talk about Positive Psychology, solution-based approaches, and strength-based work. We are talking about what works in life and the plus-side of life. Instead of merely correcting deficits and curing ills, we are concerned in those endeavors to go beyond Freud's notion that the best we can expect is "ordinary misery" out of this life and the endeavor of psychotherapy.

A recent study (Byrd-Craven, Geary, Rose, & Ponzi, 2008) showed that extensive discussions of problems and encouragement of "problem talk," rehashing the details of problems, speculating about problems, and dwelling on negative affect in particular, lead to a significant increase in the stress hormone cortisol, which predicts increased depression and anxiety over time. In this tome, we have presented a different orientation. Both of us were "converted" to this more hopeful and positive approach some years ago and have seen the good effect it has had on our clinical work, our morale, and our clients. We hope we have at least piqued your interest in it, if not converted you.

We have taken a whirlwind tour through the land of Positive Psychology and its applications to clinical work. We have surely missed some things, and given short shrift to other things. Some research we have cited may be superseded or out of date by the time it reaches print or is in your hands. (Anticipating this, we have provided a website for ongoing updates and supplemental materials that you can visit: www. therapistsnotebookonpositivepsychology.com.) But again, we hoped to get this work out to front-line clinicians and couldn't wait for perfection or forever. Please forgive us any of our all-too-human flaws.

We have tried to provide some coherent framework to organize this messy field in the P.O.S.I.T.I.V.E. mnemonic.

Martin Seligman offers a different framework, and one of our final exercises is based on that framework.

The Four Pillars of Positive Psychology

Overview

Martin Seligman (2009) has identified four "pillars" of Positive Psychology: *Positive Emotion*, *Meaning*, *Positive Relationships*, and *Positive Accomplishments*. *Positive Emotion* represents subjective well-being and happiness, including an orientation toward possibilities. *Meaning* relates to the contributions people make to things bigger than themselves and the meaning they draw from those larger contributions. *Positive Relationships* include connections people make with each other and the ways that they positively benefit from such connections. *Positive Accomplishments* represent mastery, competence, and achievement. Each of these pillars or disciplines represents a pathway to higher degrees of well-being and flourishing. The purpose of this exercise is to familiarize therapists with the four pillars.

Suggestions for Use

This exercise is primarily for therapists; however, it can be reconfigured for use with clients. This exercise provides an opportunity for therapists to familiarize themselves with the four pillars of Positive Psychology and many of the primary terms associated with each respective pillar. An understanding of these pillars, terms, and the foundations of Positive Psychology will help in choosing and implementing the following exercises in this manual.

Exercise

To complete this exercise, please complete the following steps.

1. Begin by reviewing the following areas, which represent the pillars of Positive Psychology.

   Pillar 1: Positive Emotion
   "The Pleasant Life" includes:
   Subjective well-being
   Happiness
   Gratitude
   Savoring
   Flow
   Signature strengths
   Possibilities

   Pillar 2: Meaning
   "The Meaningful Life" includes:
   Positive institutions
   Virtues
   Contribution
   Service
   Altruism
   Hope
   Future-mindedness
   Positive deviance

Pillar 3: Positive Relationships
    Include:
        Social connections
        Intimate relationships
        Positive interactions
        Pets
        Church/spiritual communities
        Professional, work, or interest groups
        Teams
        Military units
        Support groups

Pillar 4: Positive Accomplishments
    Include:
        Mastery
        Competence
        Achievement
        Successes
        New skills acquisition

2. For each pillar, identify two things about yourself that match one or more of the descriptors under that pillar.

Pillar 1
    Example: I express my appreciation to my two co-workers at least twice a week by thanking them for something they did to make my job a little easier. (Gratitude)

1. _____
    _____
2. _____
    _____

Pillar 2
    Example: I serve on the board of my township, advocating for others and ensuring that their voices are heard. (Service)

1. _____
    _____
2. _____
    _____

Pillar 3
    Example: I have two very good friends who I check in with each week and visit with in person at least two times per month. (Social connections)

1. _____
    _____

2. _____

_____

Pillar 4
Example: I recently completed my training in first aid. (Achievement; Success; New skills acquisition)

1. _____

_____

2. _____

_____

3. Identify one step that you can make toward experiencing greater life satisfaction and well-being through each of the pillars.

Pillar 1
Example: At least twice a week, I will fully immerse myself in and engage in playing my guitar for a minimum of 20 minutes.

1. _____

_____

Pillar 2
Example: I will choose a cause that will benefit an underserved population and advocate for that cause by volunteering my time.

1. _____

_____

Pillar 3
Example: I will make one new acquaintance and learn three things about that person each week for the next month.

1. _____

_____

Pillar 4
Example: I will learn how to use Microsoft PowerPoint over the next month.

1. _____

_____

4. Take time to reflect on the activities that you have planned out. Then write about the outcomes of those activities, including what influence they have had on your sense of well-being. For those activities that have been most meaningful, make a plan to continue them. In addition, identify other activities that could contribute to your well-being and overall happiness.

References

Byrd-Craven, J., Geary, D. C., Rose, A. J., & Ponzi, D. (2008). Co-ruminating increases stress hormone levels in women. *Hormones and Behavior, 53,* 489–492.

Seligman, M. E. P. (2009). *Advances in positive psychology. The evolution of psychotherapy conference.* Anaheim, CA: Milton H. Erickson Foundation.

Appendix

Positive Psychology Resources

Positive Psychology Books

Achor, S. (2010). *The happiness advantage: The seven principles of positive psychology that fuel success and performance at work.* New York: Crown Business.

Ben-Shahar, T. (2007). *Happier: Learn the secrets to daily joy and lasting fulfillment.* New York: McGraw-Hill.

Csikszentmihalyi, M. (1996). *Creativity: Flow and the psychology of discovery and invention.* New York: HarperCollins.

Csikszentmihalyi, M. (1990). Flow: *The psychology of optimal experience.* New York: Harper & Row.

Diener, E. (2010). *Practicing positive psychology coaching: Assessment, activities, and strategies and success.* New York: Wiley.

Diener, E., & Biswas-Diener, R. (2008). *Happiness: Unlocking the mysteries of psychological health.* New York: Wiley-Blackwell.

Dweck, C. S. (2006). *Mindset: The new psychology of success.* New York: Ballantine.

Fredrickson, B. (2009). *Positivity: Top-notch research reveals the 3 to 1 ratio that will change your life.* New York: Three Rivers Press.

Gilbert, D. (2006). *Stumbling on happiness.* New York: Vintage.

Haidt, J. (2005). *The happiness hypothesis: Finding modern truth in ancient wisdom.* New York: Basic Books.

Linley, A. P., & Joseph, S. (Eds.). (2004). *Positive psychology in practice.* New York: Wiley.

Lopez, S. J. (Ed.). (2008). *Positive psychology: Exploring the best in people: Volume I: Discovering human strengths.* Westport, CT: Praeger.

Lopez, S. J., & Snyder, S. R. (Eds.) (2009). *Oxford handbook of positive psychology* (2nd ed.). New York: Oxford.

Lyubomirsky, S. (2008). *The how of happiness: A scientific approach to getting the life you want.* New York: Penguin.

O'Hanlon, B., & Bertolino, B. (2011). *The therapist's notebook on positive psychology: Exercises, activities, and handouts.* New York: Routledge.

Pascale, R., Sternin, J., & Sternin, M. (2010). *The power of positive deviance: How unlikely innovators solve the world's toughest problems.* Boston, MA: Harvard Business Press.

Peterson, C. (2006). *A primer in positive psychology.* New York: Oxford.

Peterson, C., Maier, S. F., & Seligman, M. E. P. (1993). *Learned helplessness: A theory for the age of personal control.* New York: Oxford.

Peterson, C., & Seligman, M. E. P. (2004). *Character strengths and virtues: A handbook and classification.* New York: Oxford.

Rath, R., & Harter, J. (2010). *Well-being: The five essential elements.* New York: Gallup Press.

Seligman, M. E. P. (2011). *Flourish: A visionary new understanding of happiness and well-being.* New York: Free Press.

Seligman, M. E. P. (2002). *Authentic happiness: Using the new positive psychology to realize your potential for lasting fulfillment.* New York: Free Press.

Seligman, M. E. P. (1991). *Learned optimism: How to change your mind and your life.* New York: Knopf.

Seligman, M. E. P., & Csikszentmihalyi, M. (2000). Positive psychology: An introduction. *American Psychologist, 55*(1), 5–14.

Snyder, C. R., Lopez, S. J., & Teramoto Pedrotti, J. (2011). *Positive psychology: The scientific and practical explorations of human strengths.* Los Angeles, CA: Sage.

Weiner, E. (2008). *The geography of bliss: One grump's search for the happiest places in the world.* New York: Hachette.

Positive Psychology-Related Books

Buckingham, M. (2007). *Go put your strengths to work: 6 powerful steps to achieve outstanding performance.* New York: The Free Press.

Buckingham, M., & Clifton, D. O. (2001). *Now, discover your strengths.* New York: The Free Press.

Cooperrider, D. L., & Whitney, D. (2005). *Appreciative inquiry: A positive revolution in change.* San Francisco: Berrett-Koehler.

Gawande, A. (2009). *The checklist manifesto: How to get things right.* New York: Metropolitan Books.

Gawande, A. (2007). *Better: A surgeon's notes of performance.* New York: Picador.

Gladwell, M. (2008). *Outliers: The story of success.* New York: Little, Brown and Company.

Gladwell, M. (2005). *Blink: The power of thinking without thinking.* New York: Little, Brown and Company.

Gladwell, M. (2000). *The tipping point: How little things can make a big difference.* New York: Little, Brown and Company.

Johansson, F. (2006). *The Medici effect: Breakthrough insights at the intersection of ideas, concepts, and cultures.* Boston: Harvard Business School Press.

Kagan, J. (1998). *Three seductive ideas.* Boston: Harvard University Press.

Nasibitt, J. (2006). *Mindset: Reset your thinking and see the future.* New York: HarperCollins.

Syed, M (2010). *Bounce: Mozart, Federer, Picasso, Beckham, and the science of success.* New York: HarperCollins.

Journals

Journal of Positive Psychology
Journal of Happiness Studies
Emotion
Review of General Psychology
Psychological Science
Psychotherapy Networker
American Psychologist

Websites

Bill O'Hanlon & Bob Bertolino—www.therapistsnotebookonpositivepsychology.com
University of Pennsylvania Positive Psychology Center—www.ppc.sas.upenn.edu
Authentic Happiness—www.authentichappiness.org
Positive Psychology News Daily—www.pos-psych.com

University of Michigan Center for Positive Organizational Scholarship—www.bus.umich.edu/
   Positive
VIA Institute on Character—www.viacharacter.org
Centre for Confidence and Well-Being—www.centreforconfidence.co.uk
Ed Diener—internal.psychology.illinois.edu/~ediener
Jonathan Haidt—people.virginia.edu/~jdh6n/
Sonja Lyubomirsky—www.faculty.ucr.edu/~sonja/
Gallup-Healthways Well-Being Index—www.well-beingindex.com
Better Together—www.bettertogether.org
Fetzer Institute—Campaign for Love and Forgiveness—www.loveandforgive.org
World Values Survey—www.worldvaluessurvey.org

Index